Leisure Arts 21

Sky & Water in Pastel

Aubrey Phillips

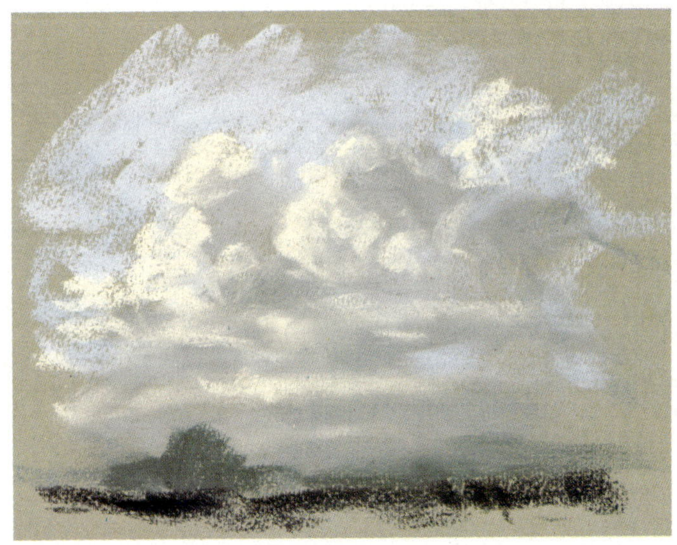

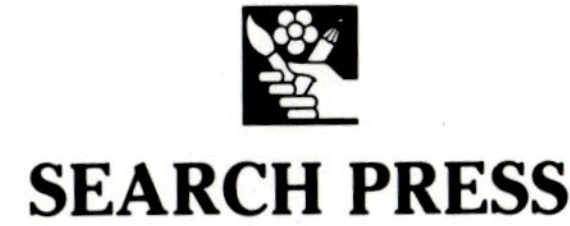

SEARCH PRESS

Wellwood North Farm Road Tunbridge Wells

Introduction

As I am primarily a landscape painter, I am always fascinated by the dramatic effect of skies, and how they affect the subject-matter of the pictures I paint. The lazy drift of broken cloud over the terrain below casts shadows on trees, fields, forests, lakes, the sea: a burst of sunshine minutes later on the same spot formerly in shadow reveals totally new tonal and chromatic values. A lowering sky dramatises what, in more clement weather, would be a gentle pastoral. Falling rain, early morning mists, sun-rises and sunsets – in short the weather that covers the subject of a picture – is an ever-changing and integral part of it. Time and time again I have gone back to a favourite spot to find it changed, by the seasons, and by the weather at that particular time.

Water, too, plays an important part in my picture-making. The division between sea and land often shows nature at its most dramatic; such as when the wind whips up the waves which hurl themselves upon rocky shores, or where a landscape is reflected in the stiller waters of a lake, stream or flooded field.

The pastel medium is ideal for such picture-making. I can work easily and quickly with it (and sometimes make up to a dozen pastel sketches in a day), my equipment is not cumbersome either in the studio or for sketchwork outdoors, and although pastels have a tendency to rub and smudge on the paper if a picture is carelessly handled, I give tips and hints in this book to guard against that.

Pastels come in an enormous range of colours and tints; most manufacturers offer a range upwards of two hundred. Most professional pastellists, including myself, keep colour charts of those sticks they prefer to use, limiting themselves to a range of a few dozen for sketchwork, and perhaps more in the studio.

I prefer to work with pastels by removing the wrapping paper from the stick and breaking off a piece about 1in. (2½cm) long. This short piece provides me with a strong authoritative mark when it is applied to the picture surface on its side, as well as a fine line when the broken end is used. As the piece wears down, facets develop which add to the range of marks I might wish to make. I keep these broken pieces in a box containing flour. This separates them and keeps them clean so that I can select each one I want to use by its natural colour and tint. This may seem difficult at first, but practice develops one's instinctive selection of the appropriate pastel stick. When the flour gets dirty, I tip the contents of my box into a colander or sieve, tap it gently to void the flour, and then put fresh flour and the sticks back into the box.

Summer on the Avon: demonstration

I have made many sketches of the River Avon in various conditions and seasons of the year. Here I re-create this demonstration in the studio from a study made where the river flows through a part of pastoral Worcestershire bordering the Vale of Evesham, near where I live.

Stage 1 (page 4)

I start with the sky using light ultramarine, laying it in quickly with the flat broken pastel stick (about one inch long) and repeat the touches for reflections in the water below. I next place the tree trunks with dark brown, then with a few strokes of dark green-grey suggest foliage to the left and lightly indicate the position of the tree to the right. I follow with a few loose strokes of mid-sap green for the main group of trees, which I repeat in the reflections in the water. Next, I apply a soft purple grey for the distance which is also repeated in the water. A stroke of mid-toned brown indicates the reeds on each bank.

Stage 2

The same colours are used to cover more of the paper, with greater pressure applied to give a positive effect. A touch of light red-grey suggests the distant river bank, with stronger treatment of the tree and its reflections to the right.

Stage 3

I develop the shapes of the trees with the dark brown pastel used on the edge to draw the branches of the willows. Next I add a mid-blue-grey and a little lightish green-grey for trees in the distance and their reflections, and a fairly dark purple-grey as a background tone to the trees to the left. A few bold downward strokes of mid-brown suggest the reeds in the left foreground. A stronger tone of red-grey is added to the distant river bank with a line of light olive and light green-grey to suggest distant meadows. Light yellow ochre is added to the sky.

Stage 4

Dark brown is again used in more characteristic detail in all of the trees with additions of dark olive and grey-greens. A warm mid-toned olive is put in for the lighter areas and these colours are also reflected in the water. Pale Vandyke brown and strokes of dark brown (with light pressure in the latter) are added to the reeds in the left foreground.

Stage 5 – the finished painting (page 5)

It is important not to overwork the painting at this stage, so I take an overall look at what I have done so far. Deciding a passage needs strengthening I do it, stepping back from the work continually to consider each stroke or accent. Light olive green is added to the right-hand side of the willow foliage to give the effect of sunlight and light greens and shadows on the grass beneath the trees. I carry out more detailed work on foreground reeds, adding light and shade and develop more movement in the reflections. Do not overwork the picture, either by blending with your finger or adding one colour over another, otherwise spontaneity will be lost and your picture will lose the moods you wish to depict.

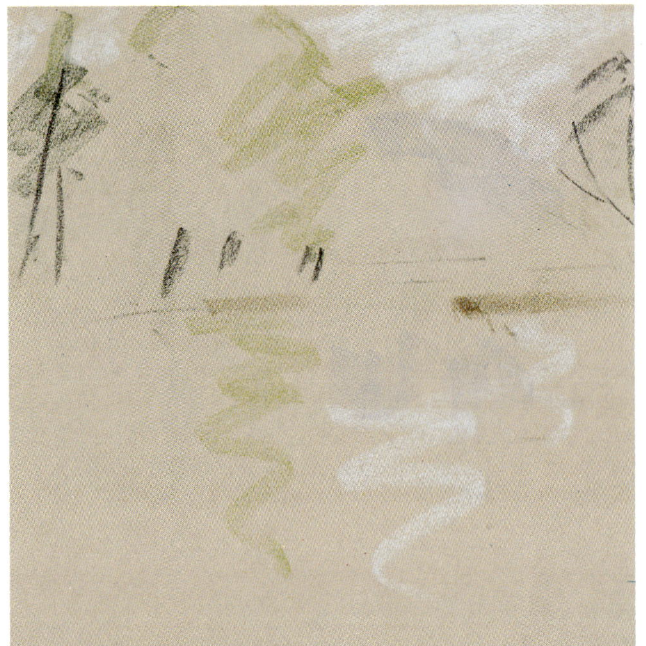

Stage 1

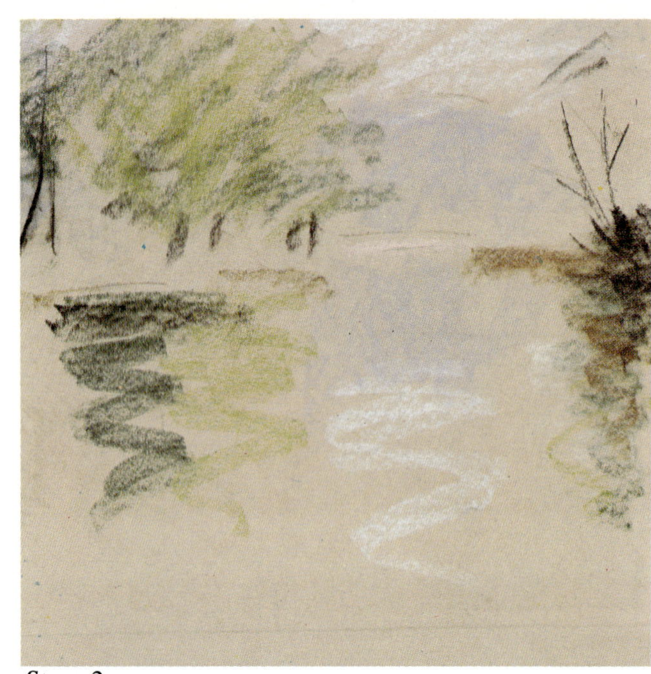

Stage 2

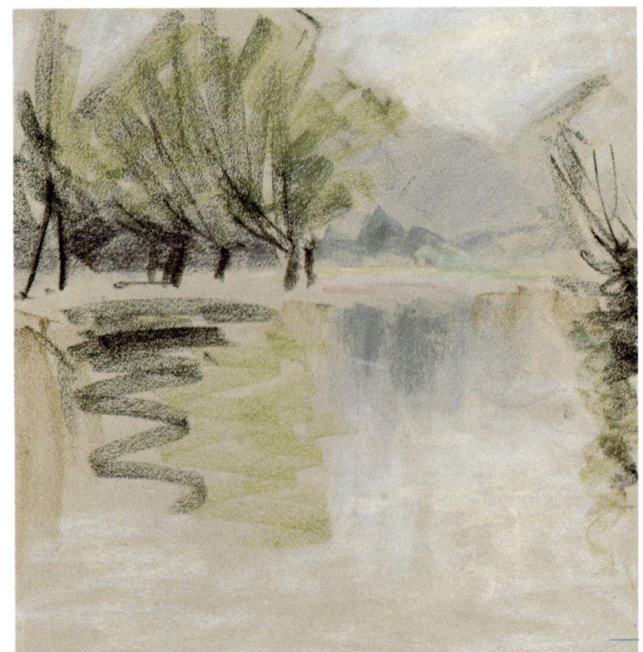

Stage 3

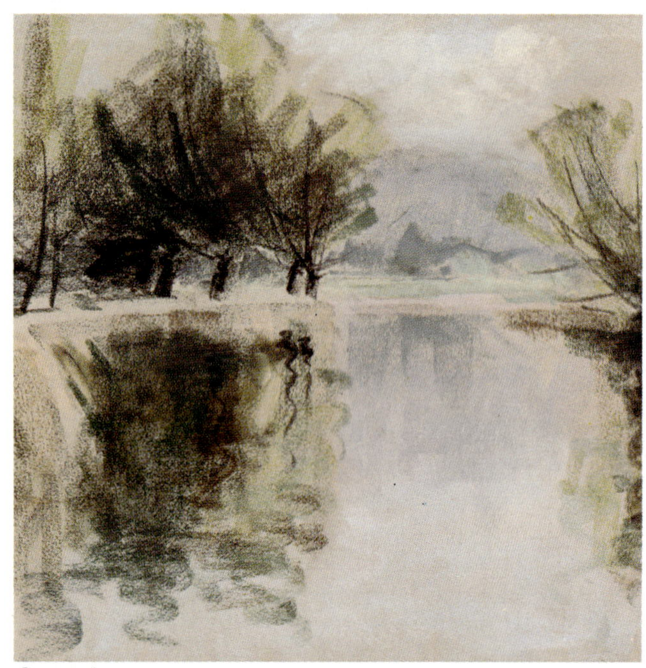

Stage 4

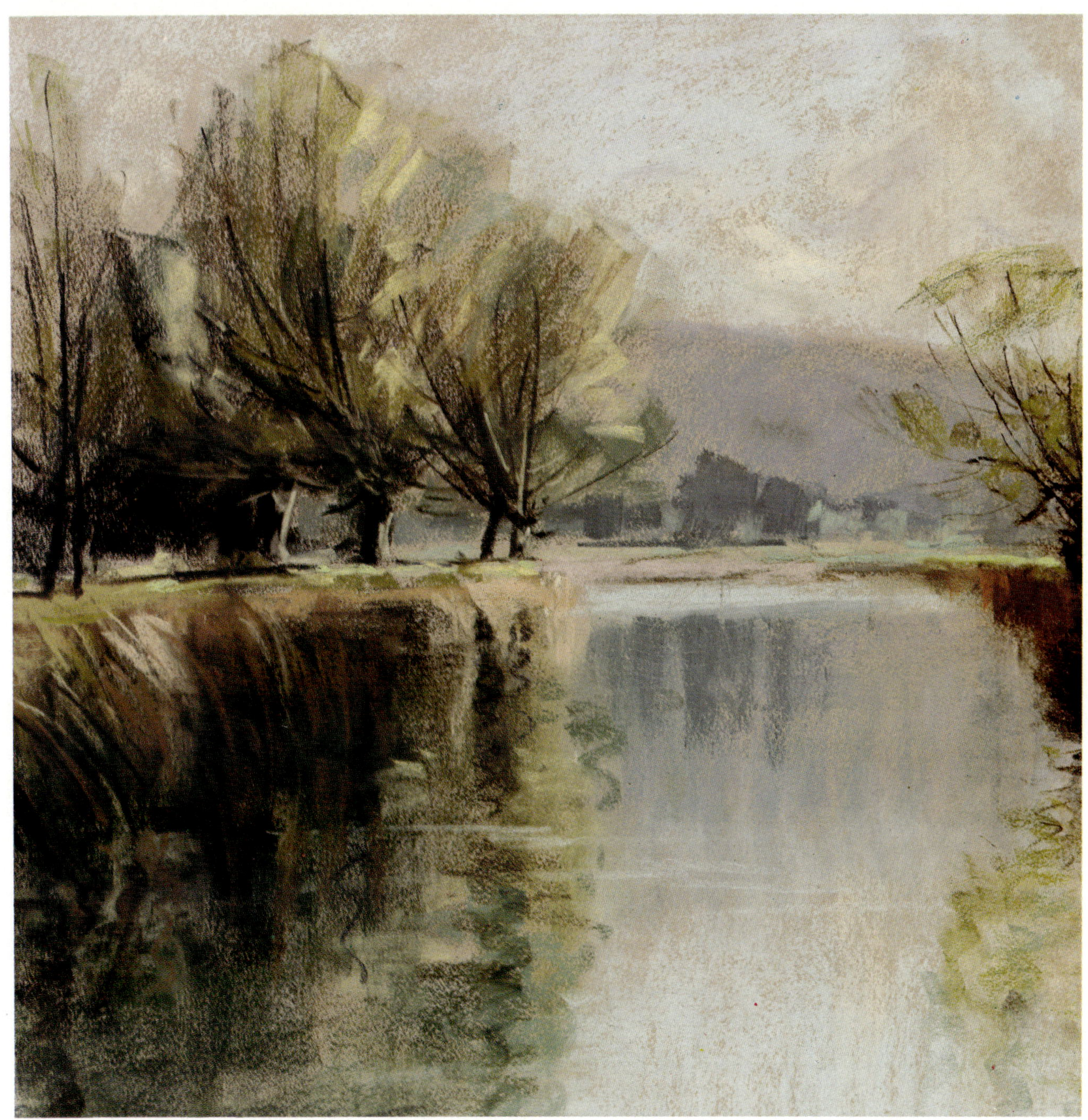

Stage 5 – the finished painting

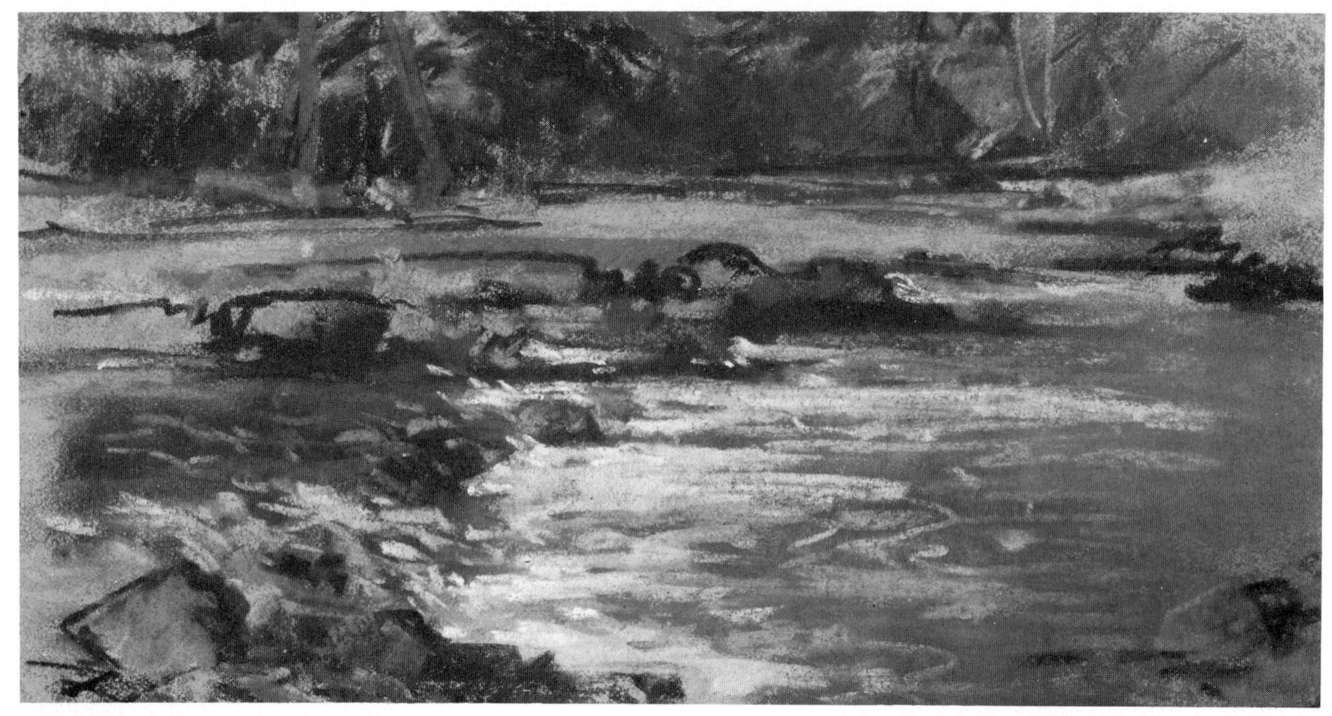

Choosing papers

The range of papers available is almost endless! So how does one choose? Consider first the end-result. It is no good selecting an extremely grainy paper if you want a soft, blended picture; likewise a very smooth paper will not provide the 'tooth' or 'bite' if you wish your marks to register dramatically. Likewise, do you want the paper to show through, to impart harmony to your picture? Or do you want to fill the grain of the surface entirely with the pastel pigment so that its support holds your marks and lines without revealing itself?

Papers for pastel painting can either be ready-made or you can prepare them to suit your purpose. Sugar paper (as supplied for schoolchildren) is excellent for sketches and even finished work. Its grain is haphazard, but it provides enough tooth to render your marks effective and the paper is soft enough for the pigments to be blended with the finger.

Harder papers, such as Canson or Ingres come in a variety of shades and have a pronounced grain which holds the pastel pigment very well. Watercolour papers can be prepared by adding beforehand a wash of acrylic or watercolour of your choice: cartridge likewise if you want a smoother surface. However before you fabricate your own support, I recommend you try out your sketches or pictures first on maufactured papers.

Lastly, there is 00 Grade sandpaper, used by woodworkers to finish off their joinery. This has (by nature) a light, sandy colour. It 'cuts' every stroke or mark you make definitively; moreover, you can fill its grain by blending or over-working to a remarkable extent. But remember, it takes a disproportionate amount of pigment from your stick, and, if you are careless, it can almost remove the skin from your fingers!

See the title page for a sketch of clouds on mid-grey Ingres paper. For a rough preliminary working on a dark brown Canson paper, see the sketch on page 16.

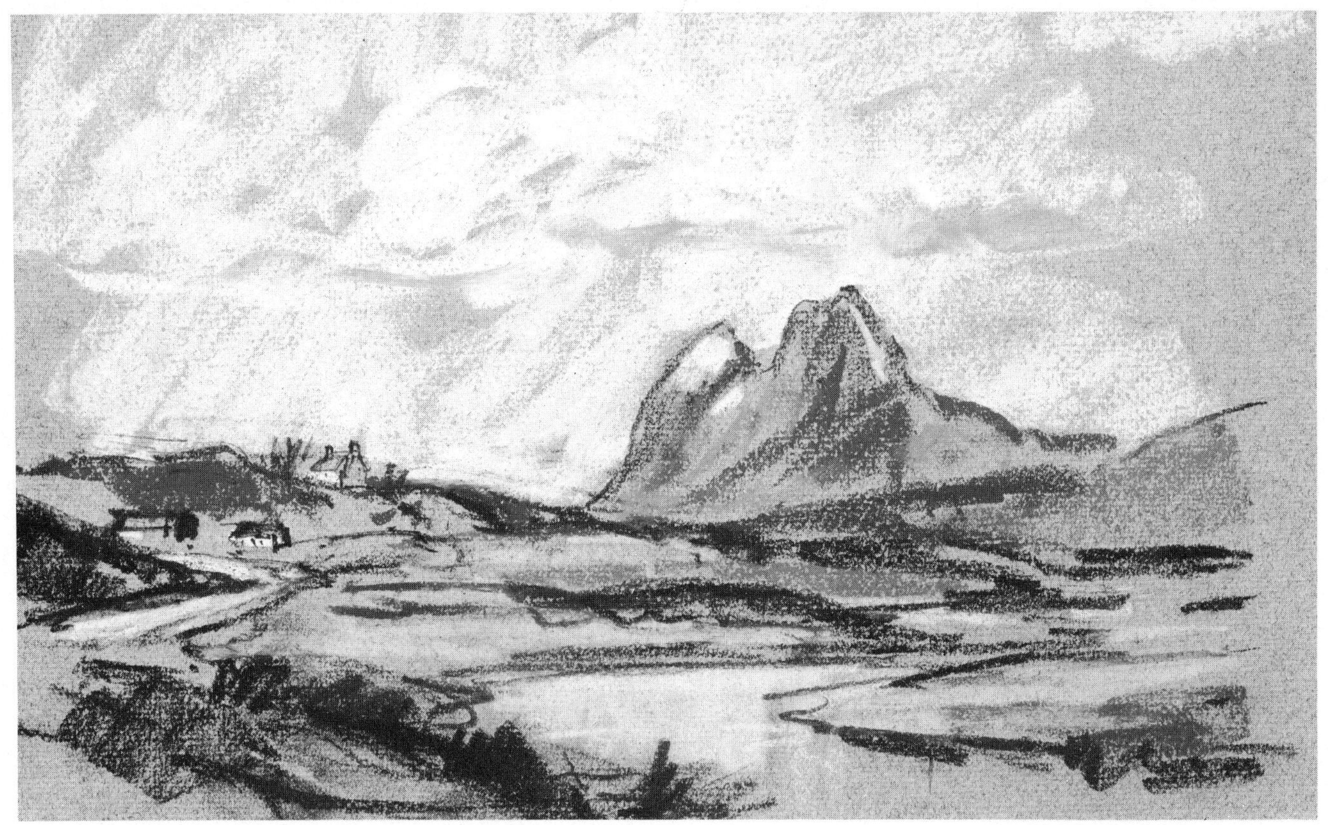

Skies

Skies and weather have a strong emotive impact on what we perceive when we go about our daily lives: they affect us emotionally and physically, the subject is part of our everyday conversation. No wonder artists are quick to incorporate the mood that the weather and sky impart into their outdoor pictures.

Before you go out to paint or sketch, check the weather reports on radio or television: the forecast will help you to determine not only what equipment you will need but suggest the most suitable clothing to wear.

The sky colours and affects both landscape and seascape. John Constable's colour sketches of the sky are small masterpieces of observation, both in substance and mood. The sky influences the ground beneath, so study the sky above your subject and relate it to what you see below. Not only will it help you choose your composition but, by observing wind direction and waiting for the drift of cloud, patterns of sunshine or shadow, you can choose your moment to make the best of your subject.

Cumulus, nimbus, mackerel sky: all these lend dramatic effect to your picture. When I go out sketching I usually know the topography of the subject I wish to depict. The unknown (and surprising) element is the effect the sky has upon it. There is no such thing as *bad* weather! Indeed some of my most dramatic pictures have originated from sketches made in pouring rain!

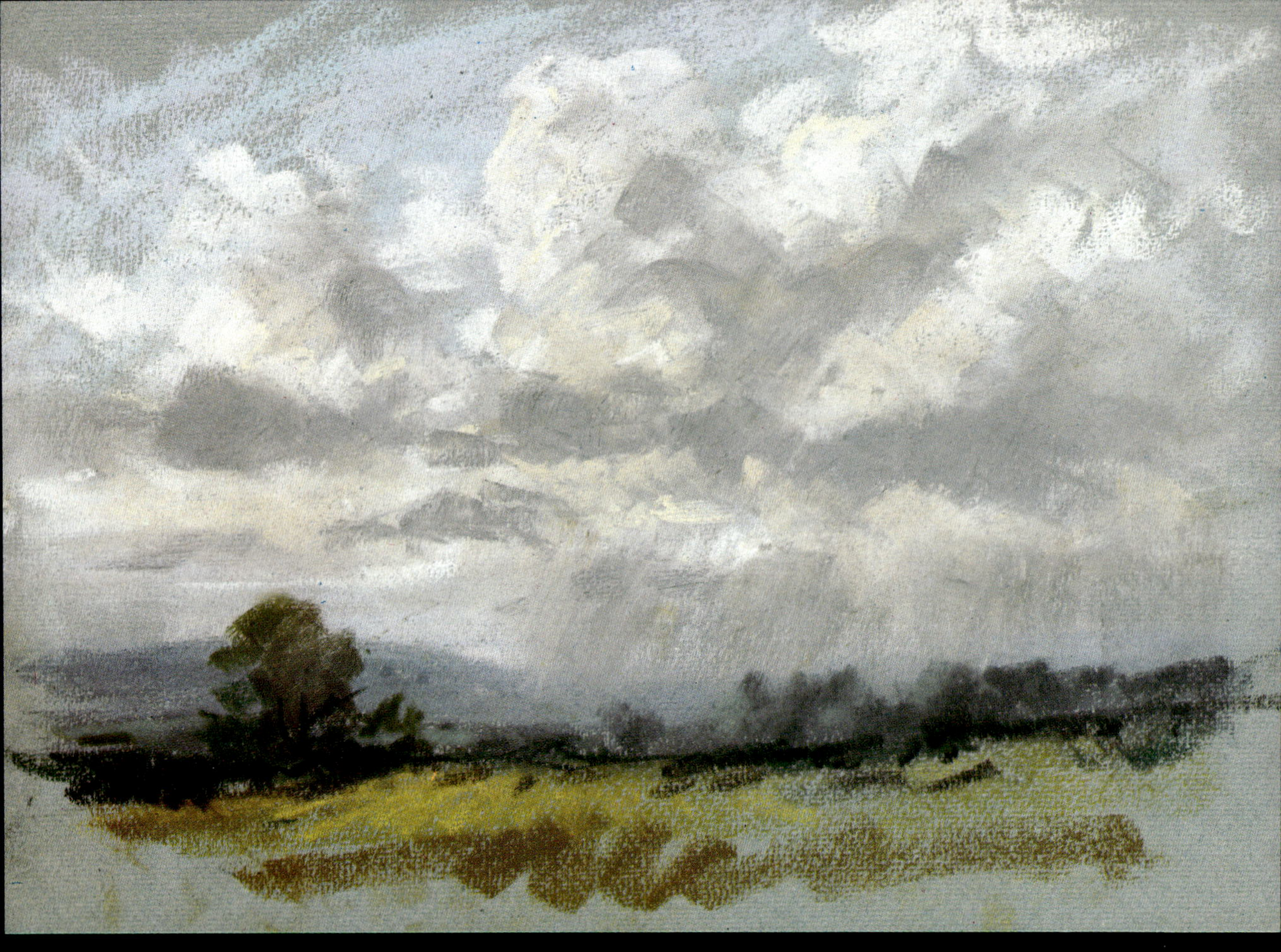

Stormy weather

Here I depict, on Ingres Fabriano blue-grey paper, a stormy effect with dark undersides to the clouds and those at a lower level wholly in shadow, together with a rainstorm on the right of the picture. In order to convey the impression of rain falling over part of the landscape area, I applied mid-toned pastels on their sides, using downward strokes, thereby softening the edges of trees in the middle distance.

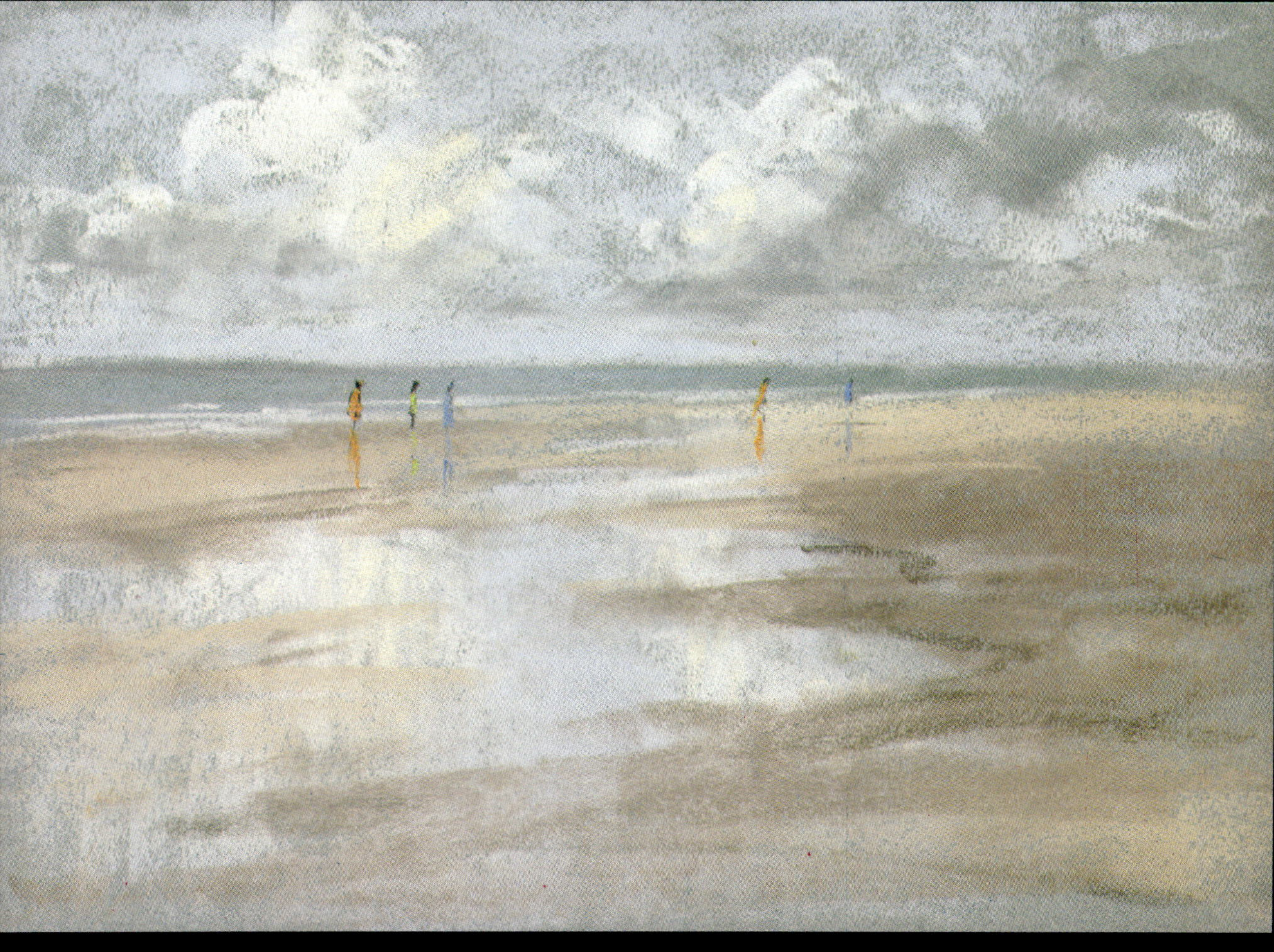

Beach scene in summer

This painting was an attempt to convey the atmosphere of a fairly calm summer day with a limited palette of soft tints, but I made use of the cool, pale ultramarine background for the sky with the grey-green sea contrasting with the warm greys, red-greys and pale burnt sienna I used for the sands.

In a subject such as this we can see quite clearly the inter-relationship between sky and landscape, with the clouds and blue sky reflected in the tidal pools on the sands. The figures, though small, play a significant part in the composition, giving a feeling of scale; their upright shapes and reflections provide a certain vertical movement to counteract the strong horizontal lines of the sea and sands. The curves and ellipses created by the tones of the sands against the pools of still water in the foreground strengthen the composition, yet emphasise the flatness of the beach.

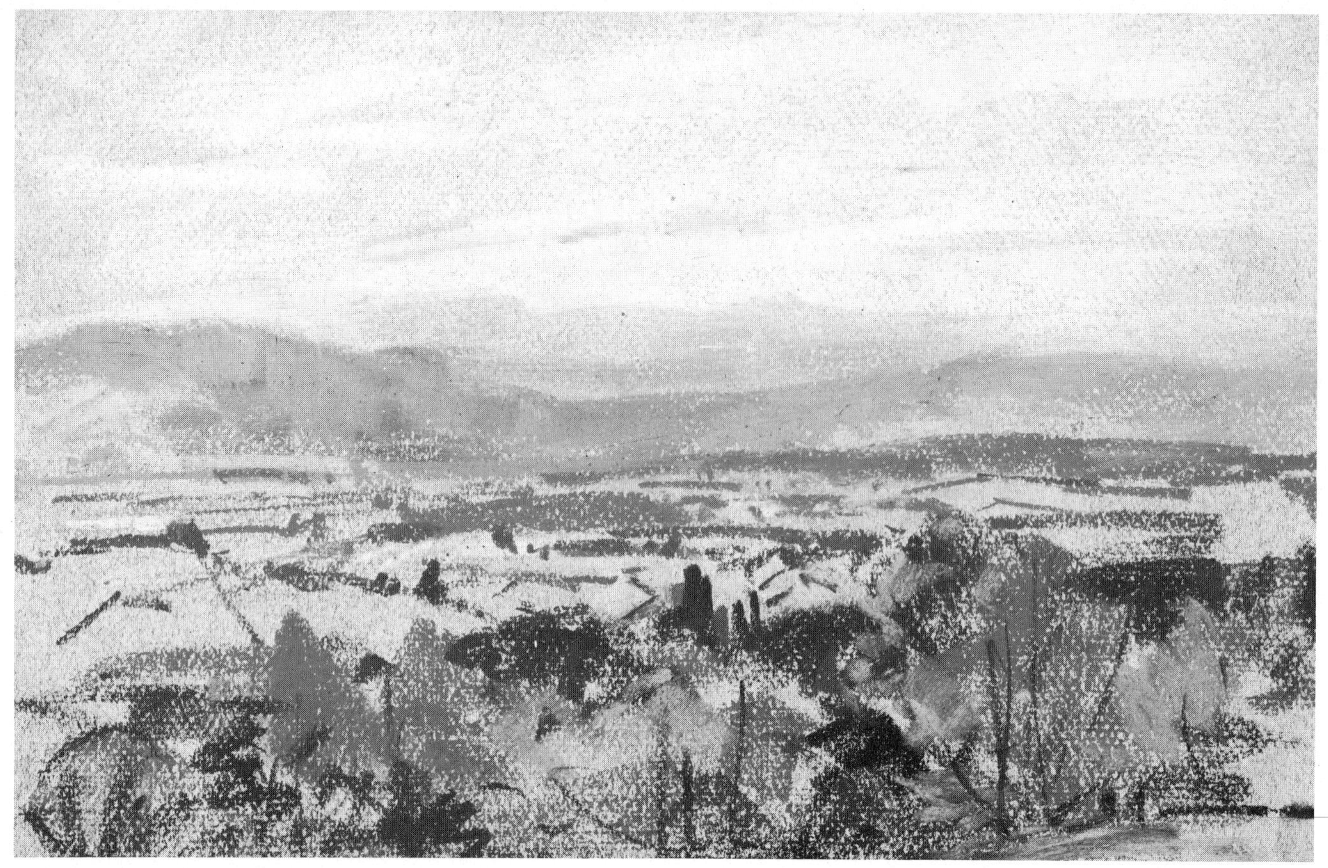

Using mixed media

Besides the variety of papers for the pastellist to work on, further variety can be obtained by combining other media with pastel.

You can start a picture by doing, first, a preliminary underpainting in watercolour (needless to say, the picture will be on watercolour paper, not soft papers like sugar or flock!). Make sure that this underpainting is dry, then apply stronger shapes, accents, detail and highlights with pastel sticks.

The way I often work is to do a preliminary 'blocking in' of my subject with black waterproof felt tip pens, usually with a coarse tip or wedge. This dries immediately and provides me with the structure I want. If I make a mistake I do not worry, for the pastel working over it will cover my felt tip marks – pastel pigment is quite opaque unless applied very lightly. I have used this method several times in the demonstrations in this book – it is quite easy to see where I have done so in the preliminary stages.

When I want a crisper effect to an almost completed pastel picture I sometimes go over it in places untouched by pigment with a fine felt tip. But, be sparing with this technique unless your subject has a strong theme both tonally and chromatically, otherwise the felt tip marks and lines will be too strident.

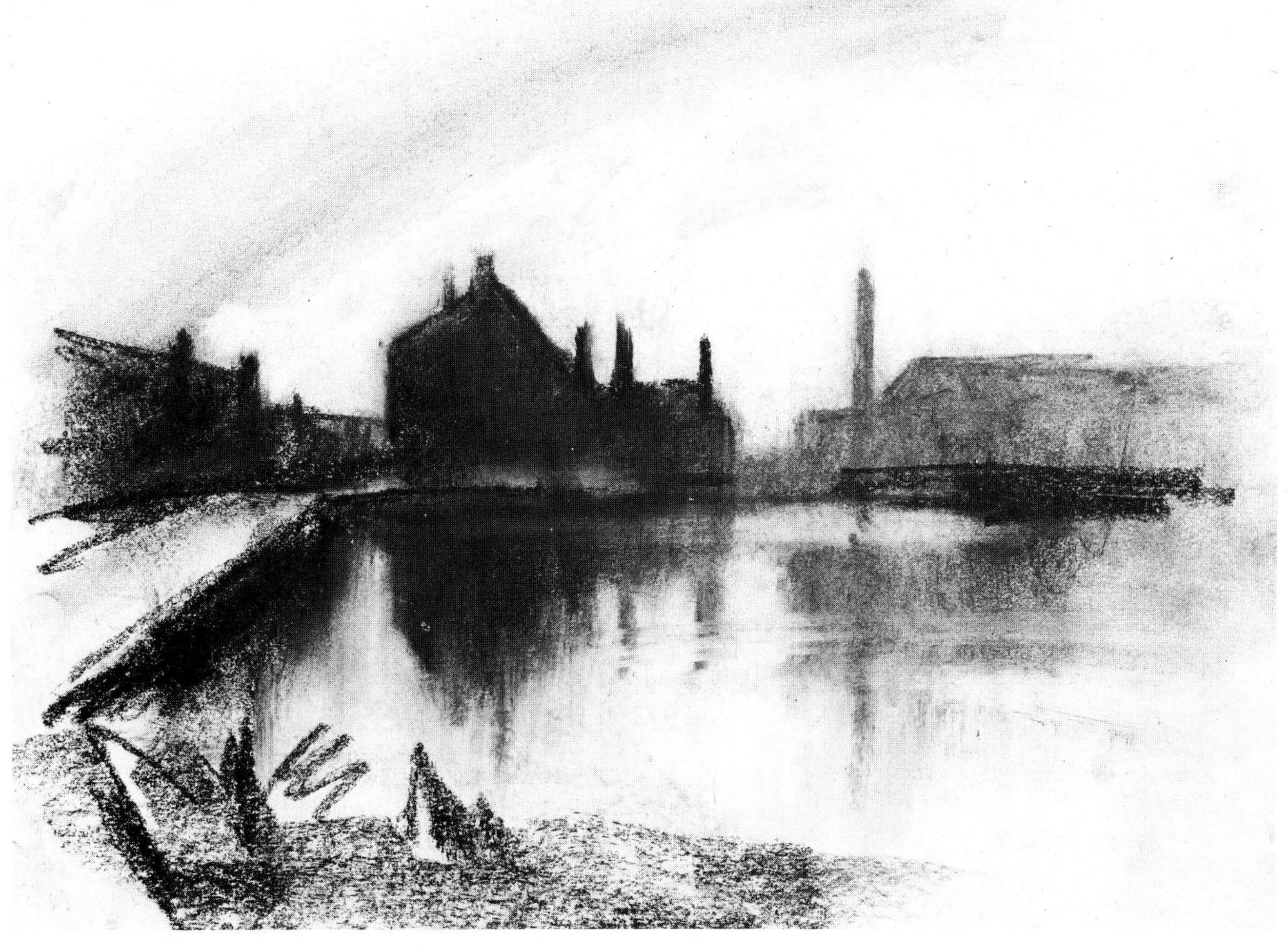

Canal scene: demonstration

The still waters of a canal often provide good subject-matter. To help me select a suitable viewpoint for this quick sketch I carry out a preliminary drawing (above) in charcoal on white paper, lifting out highlights with putty rubber.

Stage 1 (page 12)

I draw in the strong dark shapes of the buildings silhouetted against the light sky with broad tipped fibre pen on light grey Canson paper to create solid, fairly dark shapes. I then add their reflections in the water and suggest the fence and bank leading in on the left.

Stage 2

For the sky I next work pastel in broadly, with shades of light cerulean blue and warm grey, using the same

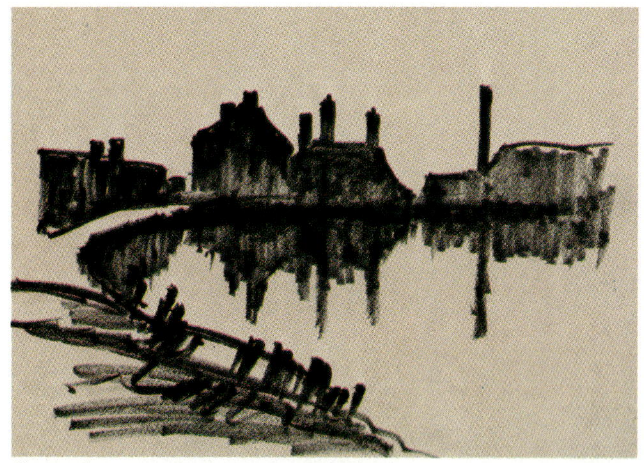
Stage 1

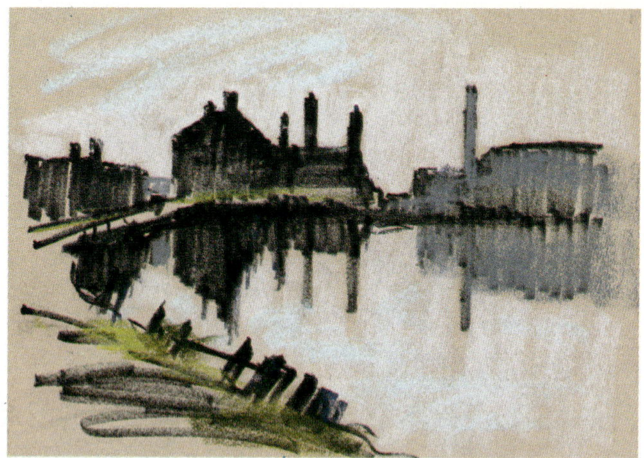
Stage 2

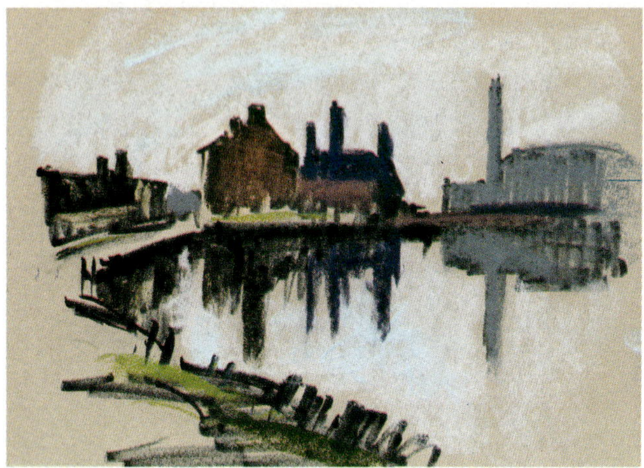
Stage 3

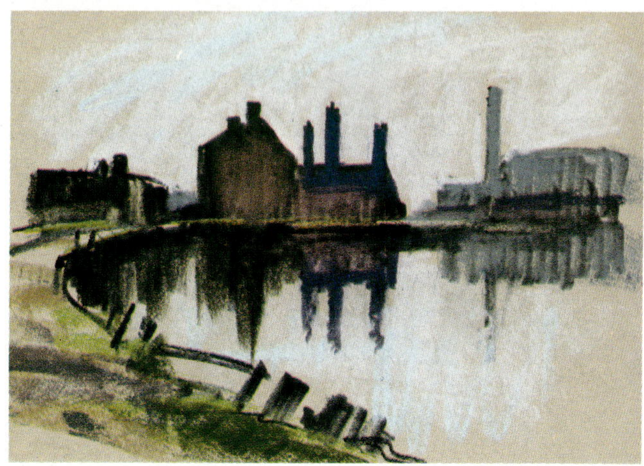
Stage 4

colours for the reflections in the water. I block in with mid-blue-grey the building and tall chimney to the right and repeat their reflections. A touch of the same blue-grey is used for the space between the buildings to the left. I then apply dark olive green with a touch of sap green to indicate the grassy foreground and the verge below the distant buildings.

Stage 3

I now use dark brown for the main buildings to the left, applying dark purple-grey for the roofs and chimneys of those in the centre. Some mid-toned red-grey is used on the walls here. A little pale Vandyke brown is applied, introducing light to the left-hand buildings. The reflections are strengthened.

Stage 4

I warm up the path on the left with mid-tones of burnt umber and strengthen up the buildings and their reflections with the same pastels as I used before. I now draw in the foreground path with mid-red-grey and purple-grey. Notice that I keep my pastel strokes strong and

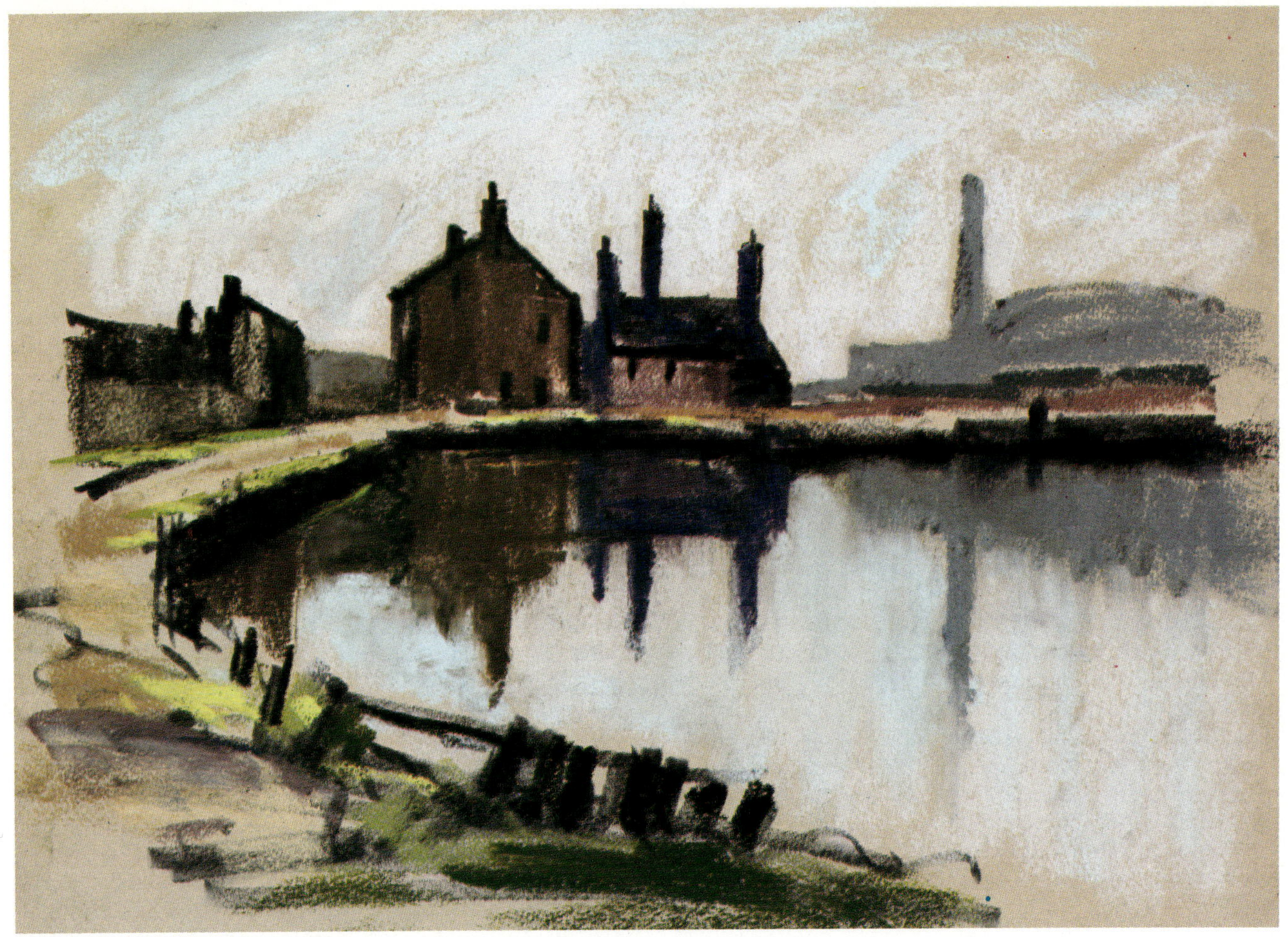

Stage 5 – the finished painting

firm; I do not blend with my fingertip but strike one colour over another where necessary.

Stage 5 – the finished painting (above)

I pull the picture together with lighter and darker accents, working on the reflections and adding light to the path on the left with pale sap green.

The whole sketch was completed in less than half an hour. I did not strive for a finished or studied picture; rather I wanted to capture in a strong manner a simple composition with highly contrasting tonal values.

Moving water

When painting water in motion, a whole new dynamic presents itself. The water's surface is broken up into ripples, wavelets, breakers, spume. Its fluidity is torn apart by the wind, by rocks as it tumbles over them or as it dashes against a rock-strewn seashore. The colour we see in moving water comes from itself, if it is muddy; from the sky, as its numberless facets reflect the lighest part of your chosen study; and from the ground beneath it. Only occasionally will the water reflect, mirror-like, the objects above it and these only in crazed half-glimpses. Even the stillest water sometimes has a band or light streak across it, breaking its mirror-like surface where a zephyr has lightly cuffed it. The minute ripples caused by the puff of wind make their surfaces reflect the sky. Magnify and complicate this effect with gravity (waterfalls and rapids), drag your water over rocky surfaces, push it against cliffs and it virtually becomes another substance altogether for the artist to depict.

The biggest problem when drawing or painting moving water is that one can never 'freeze' the motion, as in a photo. Do not try. Sit and watch it, and analyse the predominant shapes and colours as they almost re-form time and time again. No two waves are the same, but a study of fifty will tell you what a wave looks like and you will be able to incorporate it more surely into your picture.

Try to 'feel' the movement in your hand and arm when making your pastel marks. Be as bold as you dare – in this way you will render more convincingly the mood of your subject.

Waterfall: demonstration

In this study (pages 15–17) I started drawing in with a fibre-tipped pen on a fairly deep-toned, buff coloured paper, which I thought was appropriate, because the subject, apart from the water, was itself low-toned. The lighter, bright passages of the water and the distance would, I felt, be enhanced by it, as would the sunlit effect breaking through the trees. Fibre-tipped pen enabled me to establish the sharp, clearly defined shapes of the rocks, especially as they occurred against the light water and sunlit areas.

I begin to block in broadly, without detail, the general positions of the rocks and trees (see sketch, page 16) establishing clearly defined shapes and paying particular attention to the composition. Next I apply the pastels, dealing first with the distance in the upper part. Here I use light green-grey and the middle tones of blue-grey, suggesting the shapes of trees. For the nearer trees I apply three tones of olive green with a few touches of light sap green for the bright sunlit parts. These same colours were carried down on to the grass covered rocks below. For the dark tones of the rocks and nearer tree trunks I select a deep tint of autumnal brown. The light tones of green- and blue-grey in the distance were repeated in the falling water, with the addition of pale ultramarine and a few touches of white for the highlights. Brown and light green- and blue-grey provide the colours of the pool at the base of the falls.

To create the smoother effect of the rock pool with its reflections, I apply the pastels with downward strokes, before rubbing in with the thumb. The ripples are then drawn over the top with pale ultramarine and blue-grey. This, then, completes the picture as far as the pastel work is concerned but certain strengthening still needs to be done. As it is not possible to draw with broad fibre-tip over pastel, I use a stick of black conté to sharpen up the drawing of the rocks and the

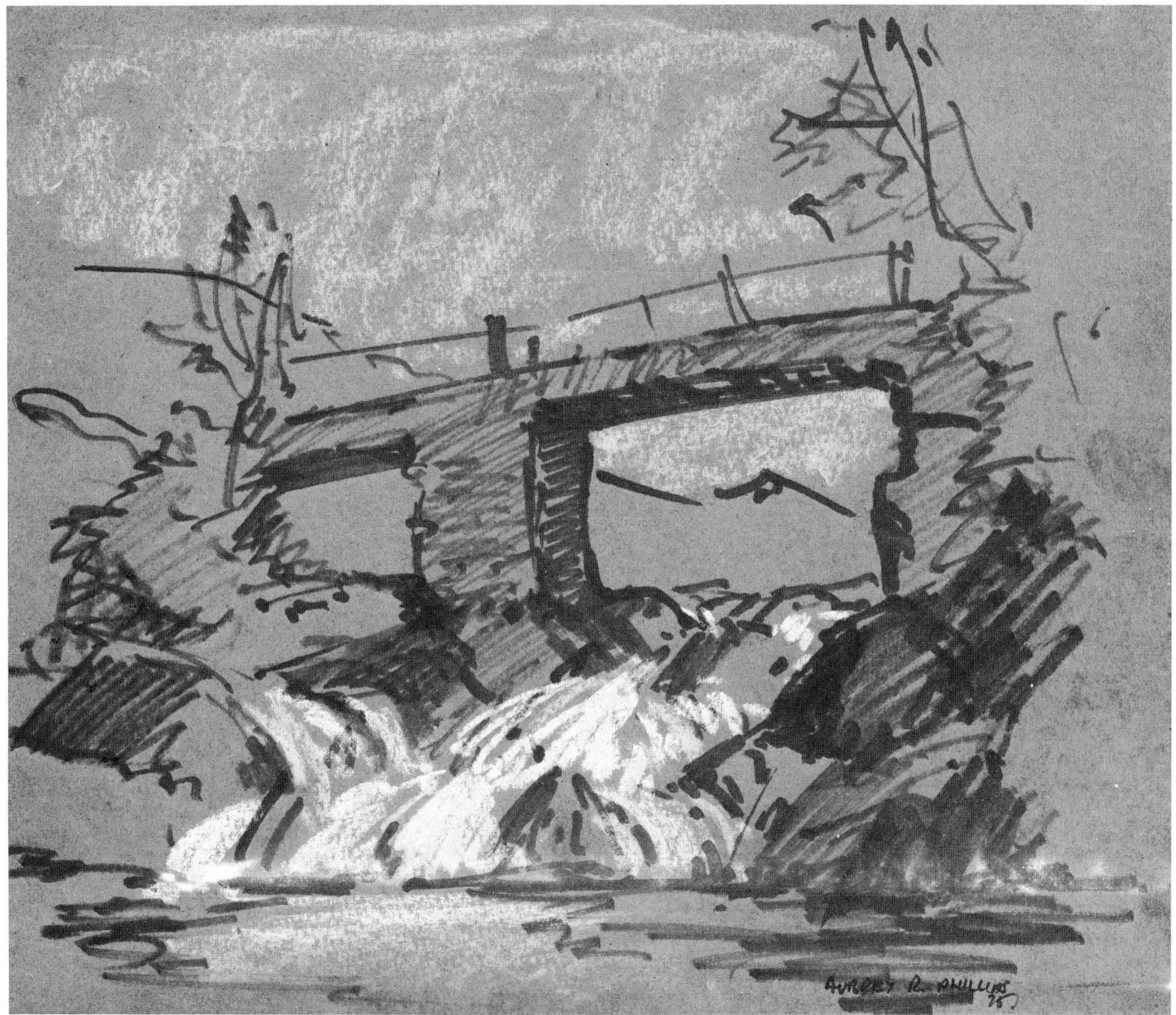

A sketch of a bridge and waterfall

nearer tree trunks, adding emphasis where required.

The warm colour of the paper has been allowed to show through and it plays quite an important part in the colour effect, as I had hoped it would. The pen work, too, shows in certain passages. About ten colours were used in the picture, including light greys and white, but I was careful not to use too much of the latter or a rather chalky effect would have resulted. The deep tones of the rocks made the colours of the falls appear lighter by contrast.

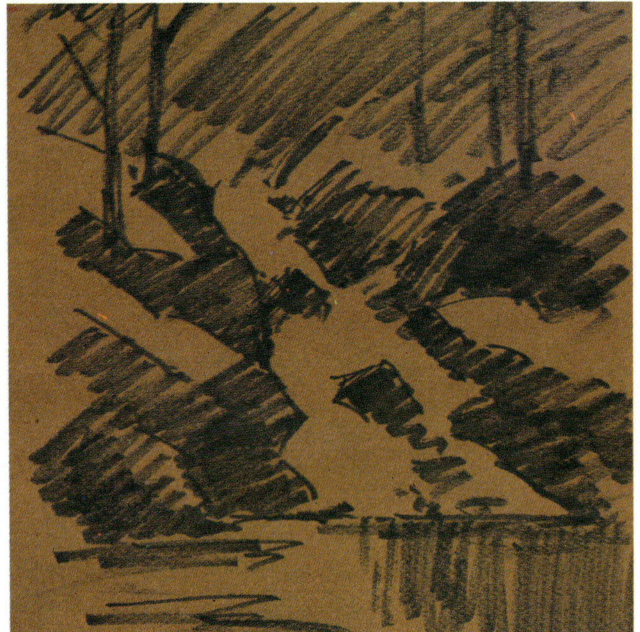

Tonal layout

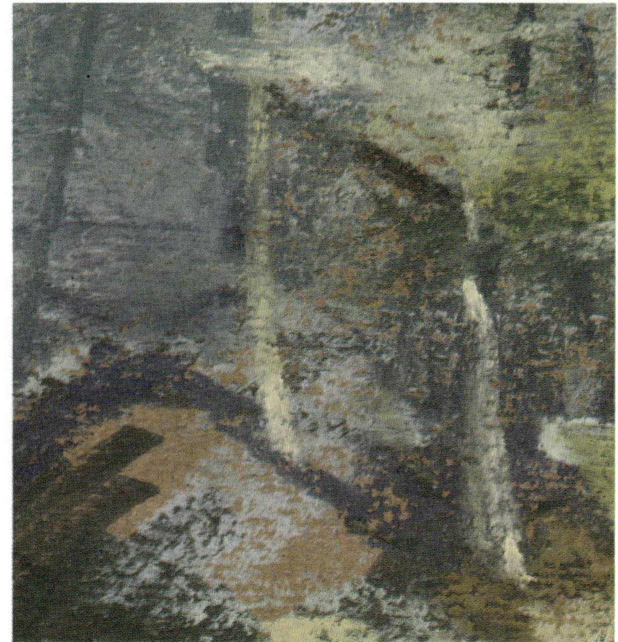

Detail 1

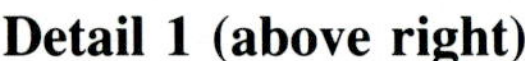

Detail 1 (above right)

Here you can see how the brown-toned paper is left untouched by pastel pigment in places. Notice too how I make my marks – I do not draw with the pastel sticks but make expressive strokes to vitalise the picture surface. This detail is taken from the top, to the right of centre.

Detail 2 (right)

Lower centre: the water tumbling into the rock pool. This is the brightest part of the picture: only here have I used a strong white accent. Most of the waterfall is depicted in cool greens and greys.

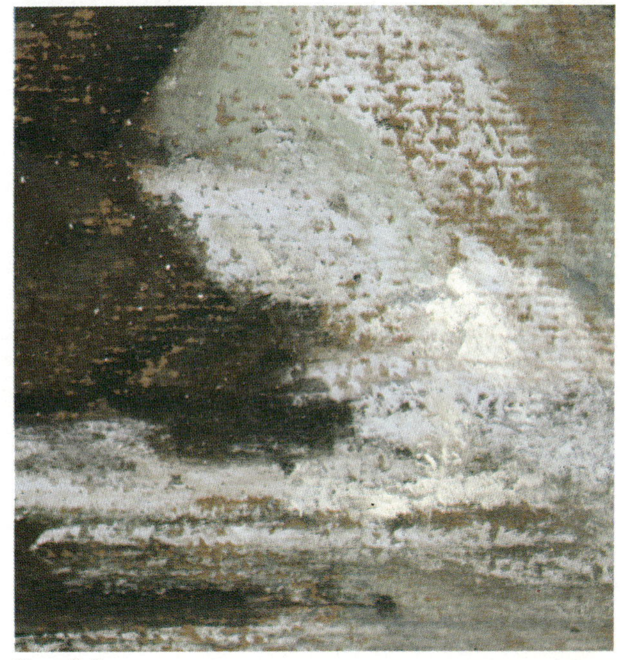

Detail 2

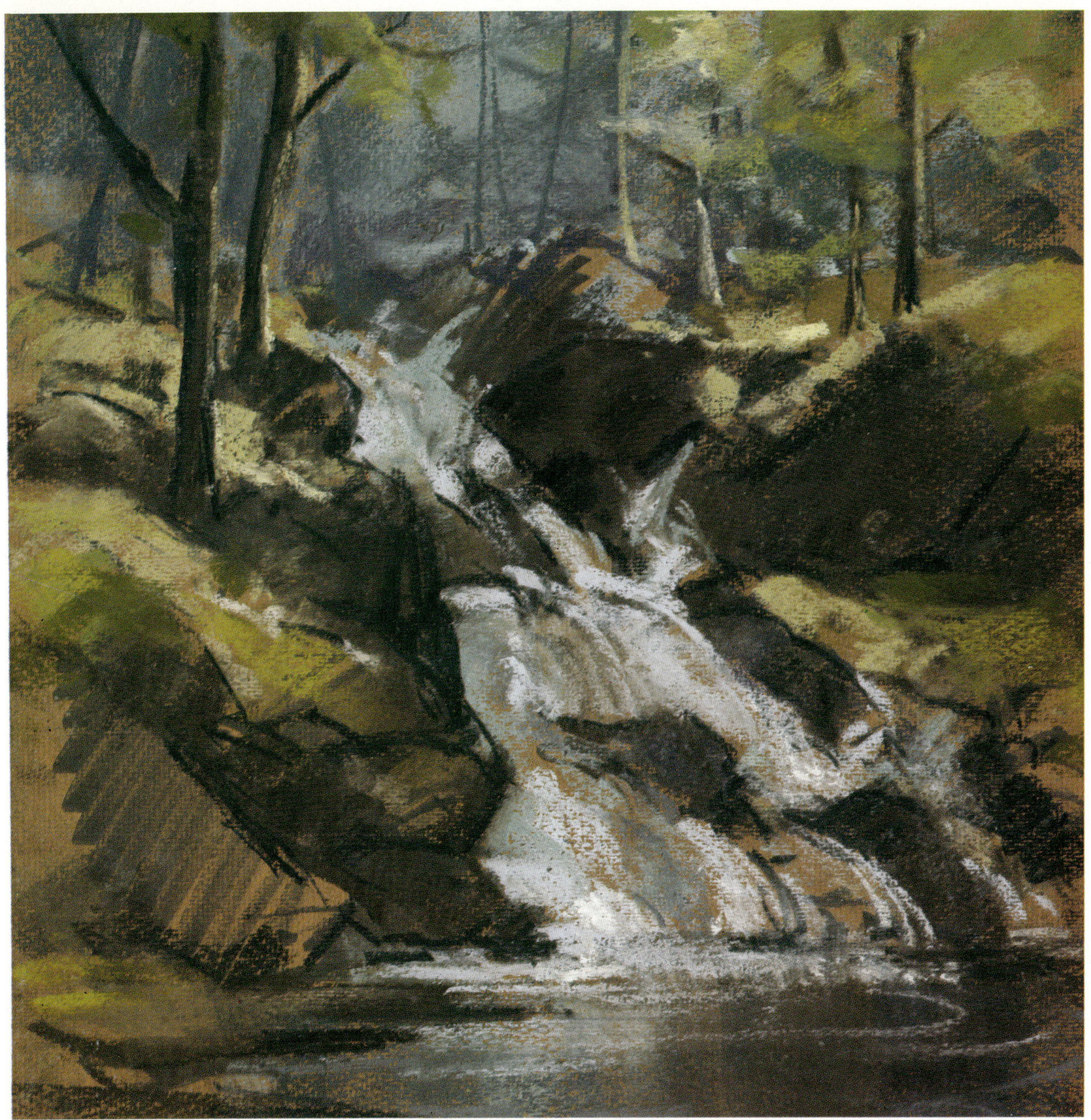

The complete painting

Boats and harbours

As most of us live inland, we often like to take our holidays by the sea or make day trips to the coast, visiting ports and fishing villages. I am lucky enough to have a painter son who has fled the city to live and work in a tiny fishing village in northern Scotland, on the Sutherland coast.

One of the attractions of small ports and harbours is the wealth of functional detail which abounds. Boats, both in and out of the water, provide attractive shapes to enliven a coastal scene. Stone, brick and iron piers and jetties add striking features to one's compositions. If you enjoy painting detail, then the fishing nets, lobster pots and all the impedimenta and equipment related to working boats will give you never-ending material. The working people there wear brightly coloured oilskin suits and sou'westers: likewise their boats are often painted in bright colours. Buildings, warehouses and lighthouses about the shore: even a large industrial port – with its ocean-going cargo vessels, attendant cranes, lorries, trucks and railway sidings – all provide plenty of scope for the artist. But remember, be careful of trespassing. If you particularly want to choose a special viewpoint which might be from a boat or inside a dock, always ask permission beforehand.

The harbour at sunset: demonstration

The conjunction of sunset and seascape has provided innumerable artists with some of their finest subjects. Turner was obsessed by sea and sky and a large proportion of his studies were made at sunset. For this demonstration I have chosen a typical Scottish inlet. The tide is out, the sun is setting behind veils of cirrus, and an assortment of working and pleasure craft lie stranded upon sandy shores.

Stage 1

As my subject was warm in colour I chose a mid-grey Canson paper with little tooth. Using a broken stick of dark brown on its side I first block in the main shapes very lightly to suggest the main tonal values, then draw in with the same stick the boats, buildings and figures.

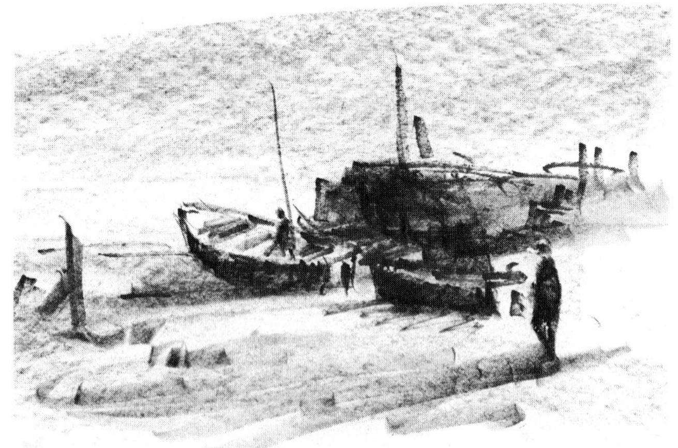

Studies such as this – made with a fibre-tipped pen on white cartridge paper with charcoal being applied for the half-tones over the whole drawing – can be useful for including in a picture of a beach or a harbour and for balancing a composition.

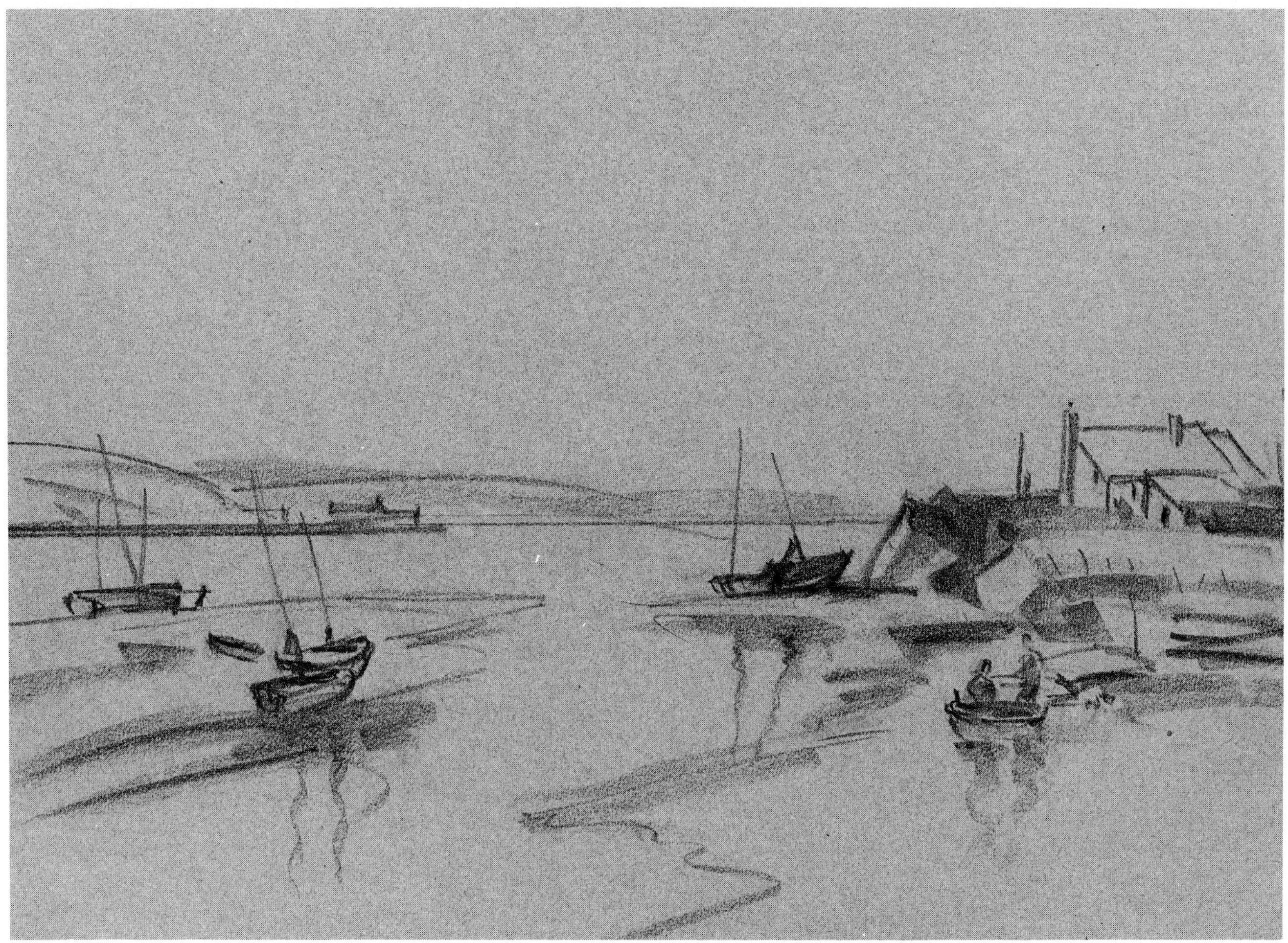

Stage 1

Stage 2 (page 20)

I now work on the sky, using light tints of ultramarine, yellow ochre, red-grey and crimson, blending them together with my fingers to create a soft effect. I repeat these in the sea's reflection, adding pale blue in the creek in the foreground. I apply blue-grey to the distant headland, thus building up the chromatic values of the picture as a whole.

Stage 3

I work more light pink tones into the sky, blending into the existing pastel with my fingers. I strengthen the distant headland, and use a very pale ochre to suggest the sandy foreshores. I also make the sea reflect more accurately the sky colours.

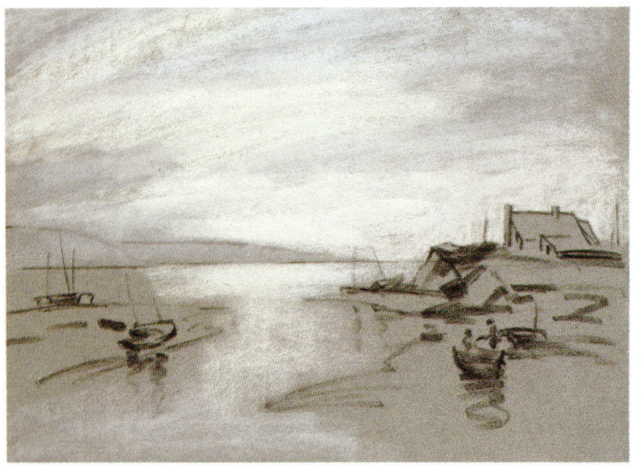

Stage 2

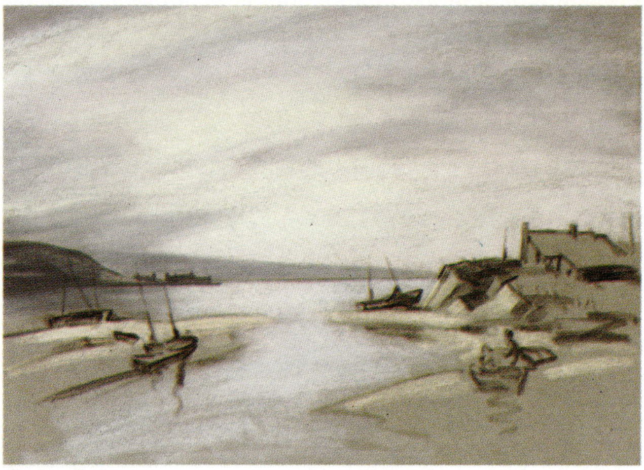

Stage 3

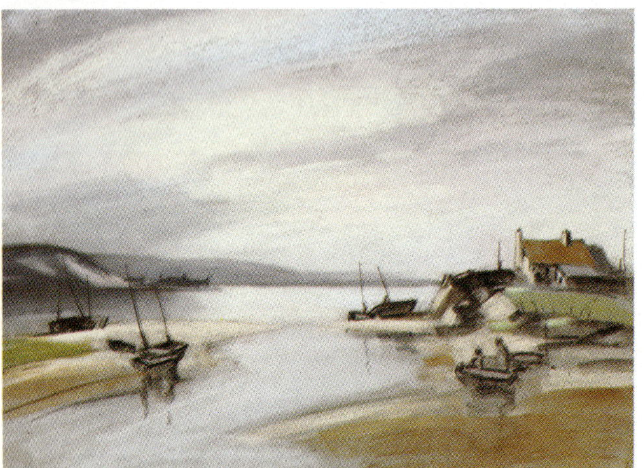

Stage 4

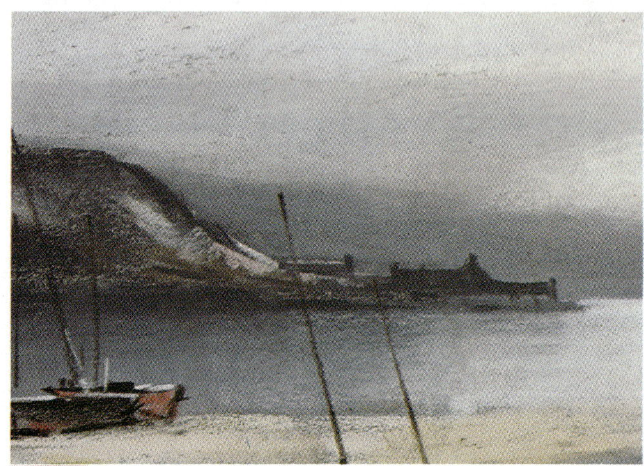

Detail

Stage 4

The sky has caught the headland in the middle distance, so I add touches of light crimson and light yellow ochre. I block in the grasses on the left and right of the picture with mid sap green, and start suggesting the darker foreshore tones with mid-burnt umber tint. I use the same colour for the cottage roof, adding blue-grey to the roofs of the outhouses attached to it.

Detail

I have picked out this area to show where I blended the pastel tints with my fingers, and where I deliberately made strong pastel strokes.

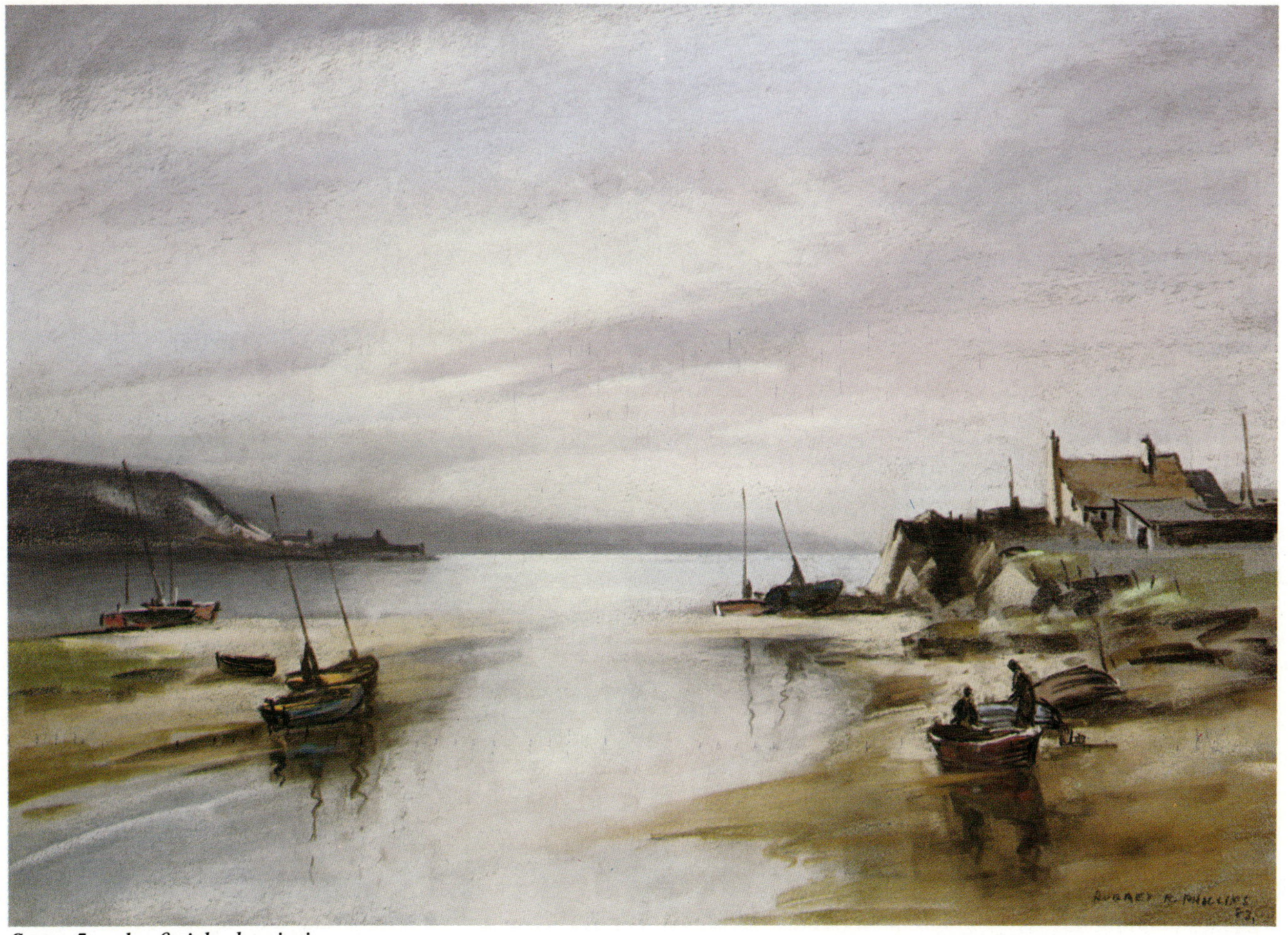
Stage 5 – the finished painting

Stage 5 – the finished painting

I now put in the chromatic accents of the picture in strong lines of crimson, orange and Prussian blue, draw in the figures almost as silhouettes and add brighter touches of light sap green to the grasses. I add reflections of the boats in the still water, and the muddy strand to the right. A little olive green is added to the foreshore. Lastly I go over the whole picture with touches of autumn brown to crispen up the details, and strengthen the rocky promontory above the figures.

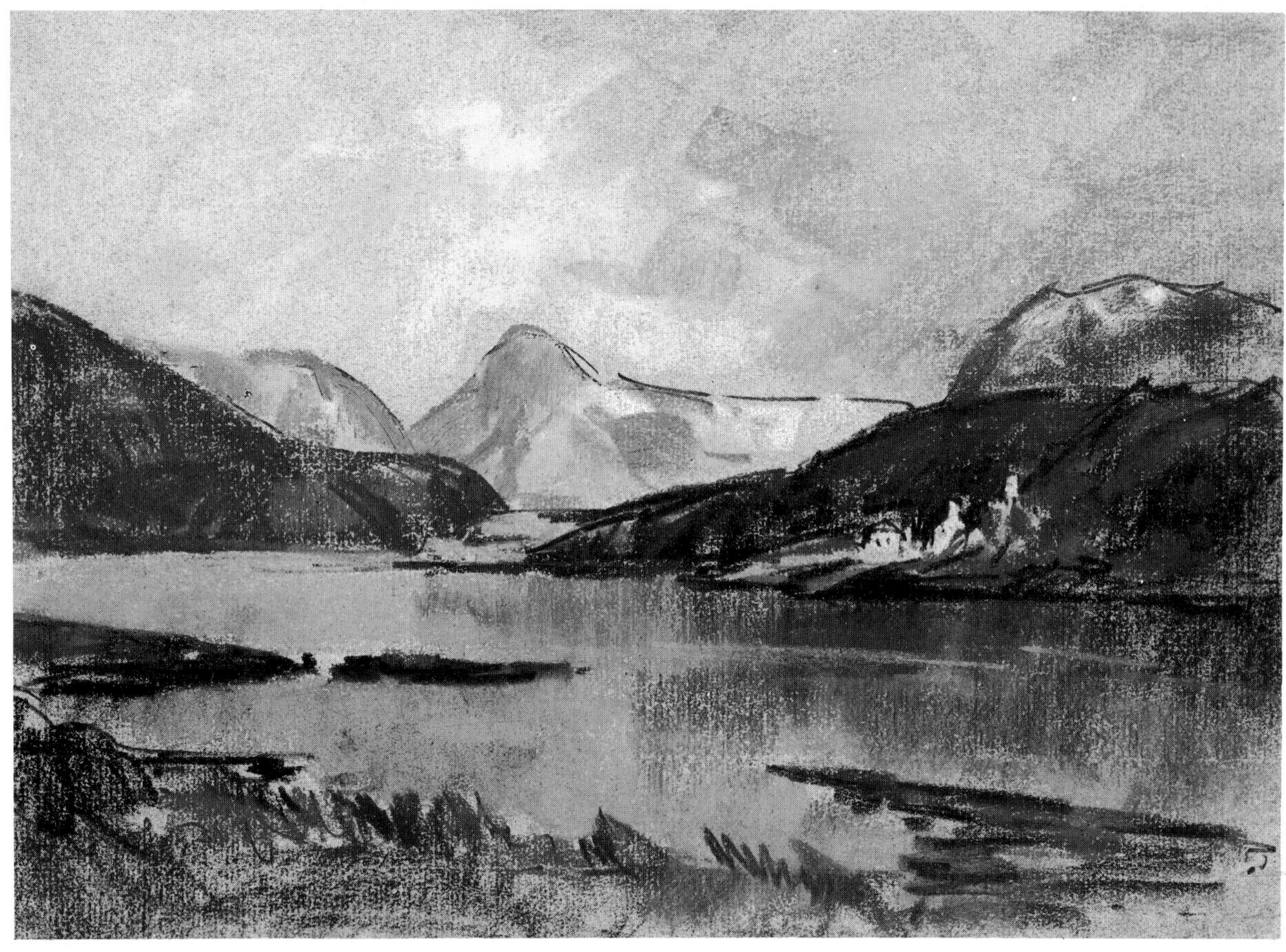

Mood and atmosphere

Both mood and atmosphere can often be most effectively rendered not only by the tonal and chromatic values we use but also by the actual marks we make with the pastel sticks. The two pictures on these pages represent changes of handling style to suit their respective subjects.

View from Kylestrome, Sutherland

The sky was almost overcast except where a fitful sun broke through to illuminate the distant mountains. My pastel strokes were sharp and angular over a grey Canson paper. I drew in the outlines of my composition beforehand in fine black felt tip pen, which reveals itself in a number of places.

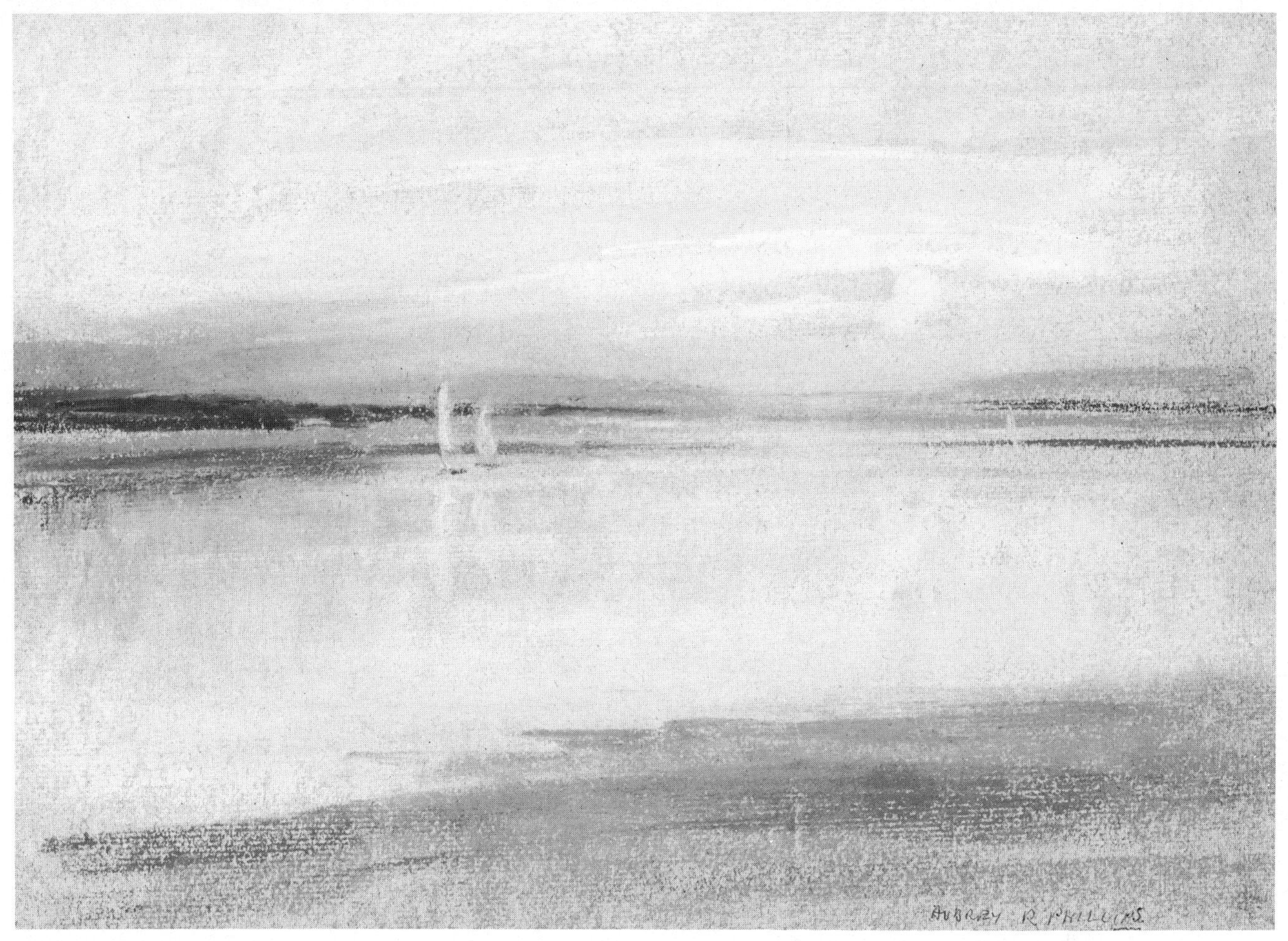

Sunset, Aberdovey

I worked directly on to warm grey Canson paper without preliminary drawing, blending the colours quickly with my fingers in the sky and water. As I wished to convey tranquillity, very little detail is put in – even the two becalmed sailing boats are only suggested.

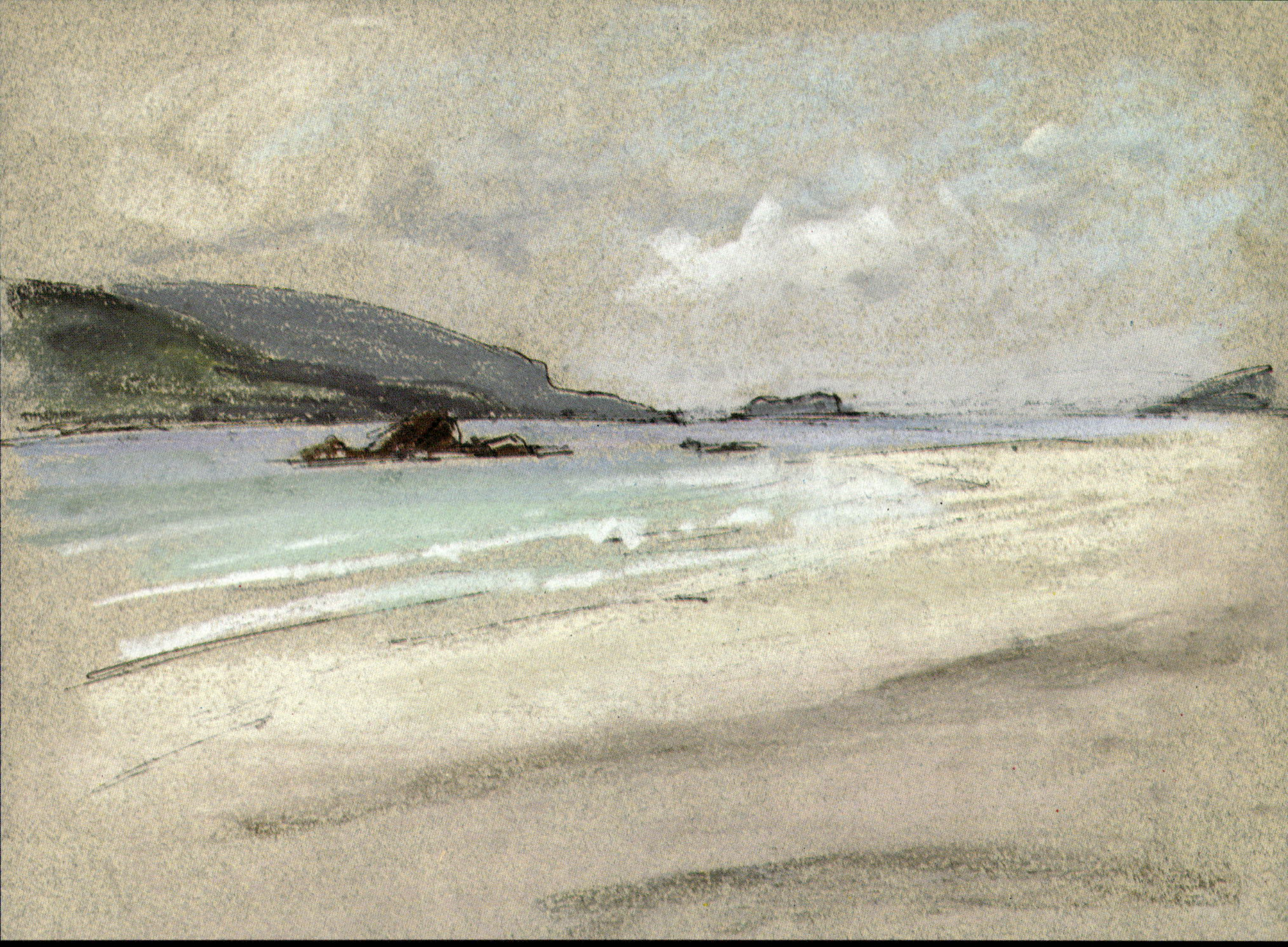

The beach, Sutherland

I chose this picture of a calm seashore in Sutherland to illustrate an important point. The ground underneath water (especially when the water is shallow) will affect its colour. In this sketch the sun was brilliant in the foreground. As the gently sloping sand met the shoreline, so the sun, shining through the sea, cast the sand's reflection up through it, changing the colour to bright green. Further out the sea reflects the sky with cool grey tones.

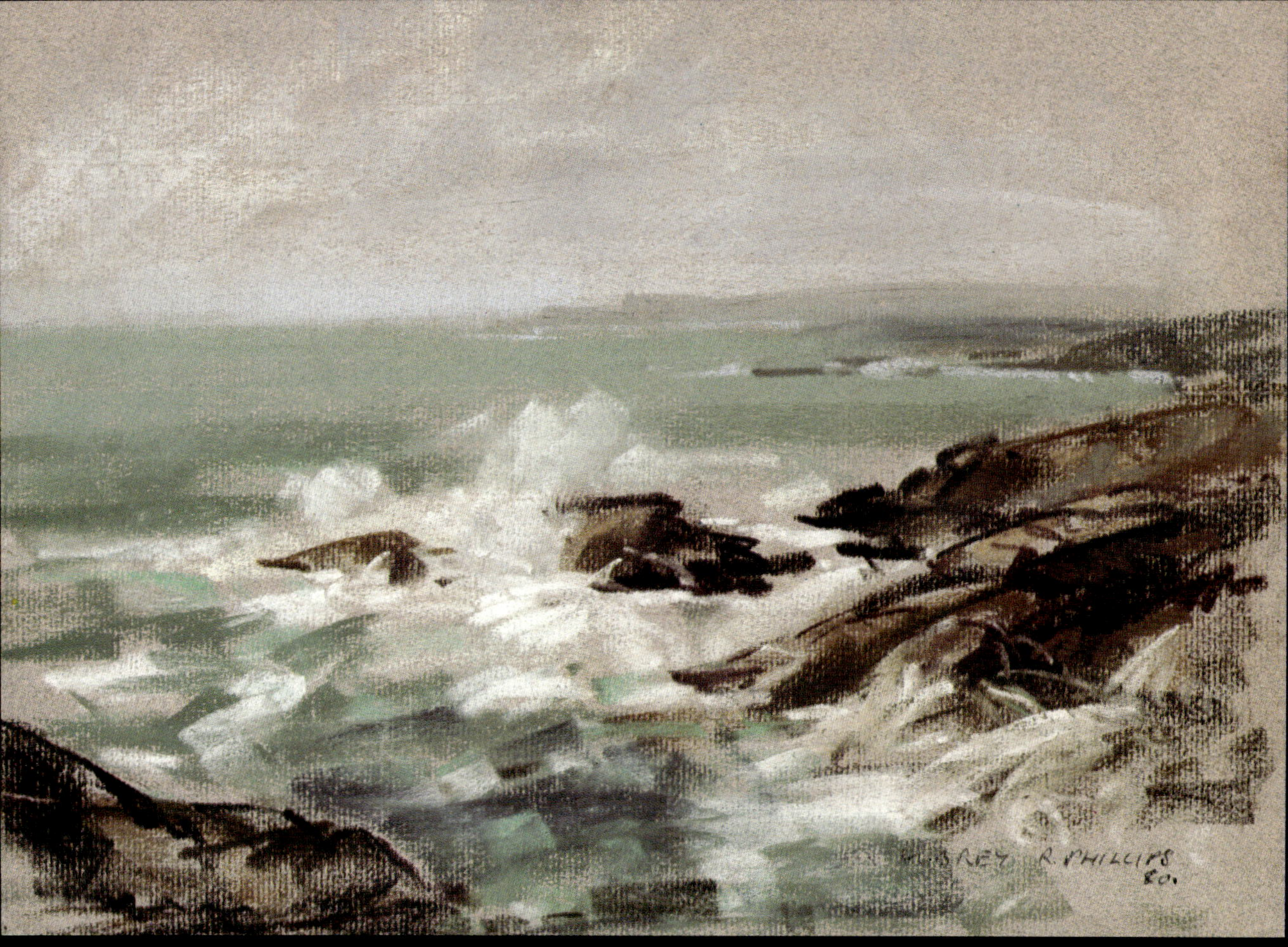

Rocky shore, Sutherland

By contrast with the mood of the picture opposite, this rough seascape was overcast with cloud, and the breakers were rolling in to crash in spume on the rocks. I sat for quite a while just observing, watching each wave break and recede before I made up my mind which moment I wanted to catch. I chose but a few colours – greens, blues, greys, dark crimson and Vandyke brown. The paper is the grainy side of a sheet of grey Canson. I wanted each mark to express the vigour of the scene, so I used broken sticks on their sides in short, powerful strokes, overlapping them in places.

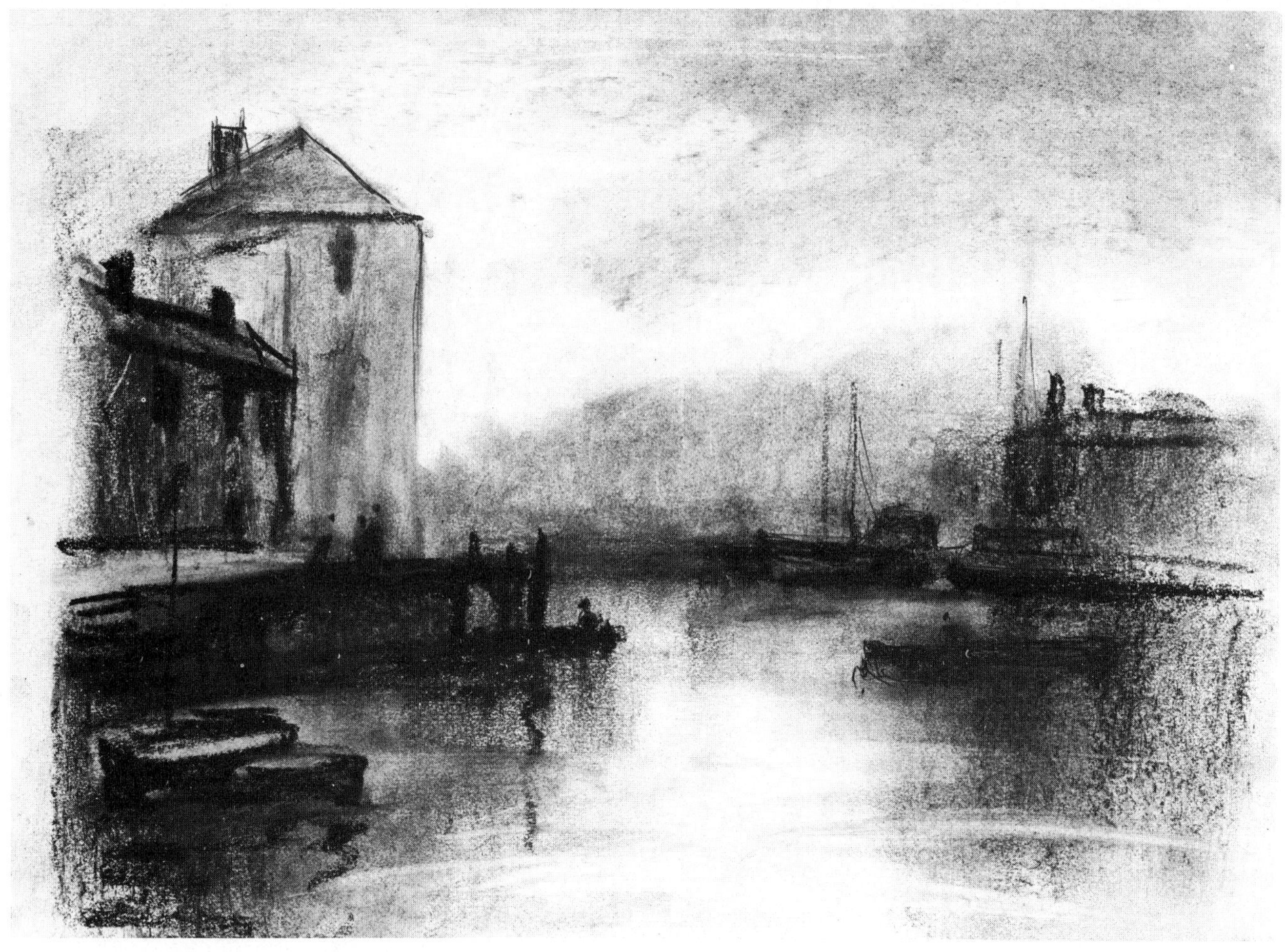

Night scenes

When daylight is ended, most painters, both professional and amateur, put away paints and pastels to carry on other activities. But there are occasions when, with the moon at its brightest or streetlights and illuminations from windows in houses and factories gleaming in sharp or occluded glow, a dramatic picture presents itself to us. Photographers have rendered the night scene so effectively that we accept their pictures as commonplace in illustrated magazines and books. I sometimes think it a pity that artists lag behind photographers in this respect.

It goes without saying that the limitations of working with pastel at night are self-evident. Yet, armed with a camera and tripod and good colour film (transparencies are best), you can record a night scene and, with a few quick sketches or notes on a pad, capture the *emotion* you felt which your photographs will help you recollect when reconstructing your night scene in the studio or workroom.

Night scene: demonstration

Harbour reflections

This is a composite picture which I made up from memories of visiting an old fishing port.

Stage 1 (page 28)

I choose a light pearl grey Canson paper and stretch it on a drawing board as for use with watercolour, this being necessary to prevent cockling for I intend to apply ink washes to it. Using Indian ink diluted with distilled water and a 3-inch flat watercolour brush, I boldly shape up the tall building on the left in a fairly dark tone, carrying the wash down to the bottom of the paper. Adding more water to the ink, I now apply the lighter area to the right, softening the edges with a sponge but at the same time leaving the shape of the left-hand building fairly clearly defined, except at the top left, which I again soften with the sponge. While the ink is still wet I set the drawing board at a slope of about ten degrees and add more ink to the right, using a rather darker tone than before. I now leave the drawing board in position and allow the ink to dry.

Stage 2

The preliminary dark washes of ink have given me a strong basic tone upon which to work, helping me to create a night-time atmosphere. I now begin to apply the pastels in pieces about an inch long used on their sides. Firstly, I use light ultramarine against the edge of the tall building with a grey of a slightly darker tone to the right and a yet still darker tint along the top of the sky (which is repeated in the water). A light touch of yellow ochre indicates the position of the moon, and its reflection in the water. I apply dark and mid-toned green-grey to the water, which I rub in with my thumb. I lay in now a dark purple grey with a dark brown to suggest freely a few shapes of the boats.

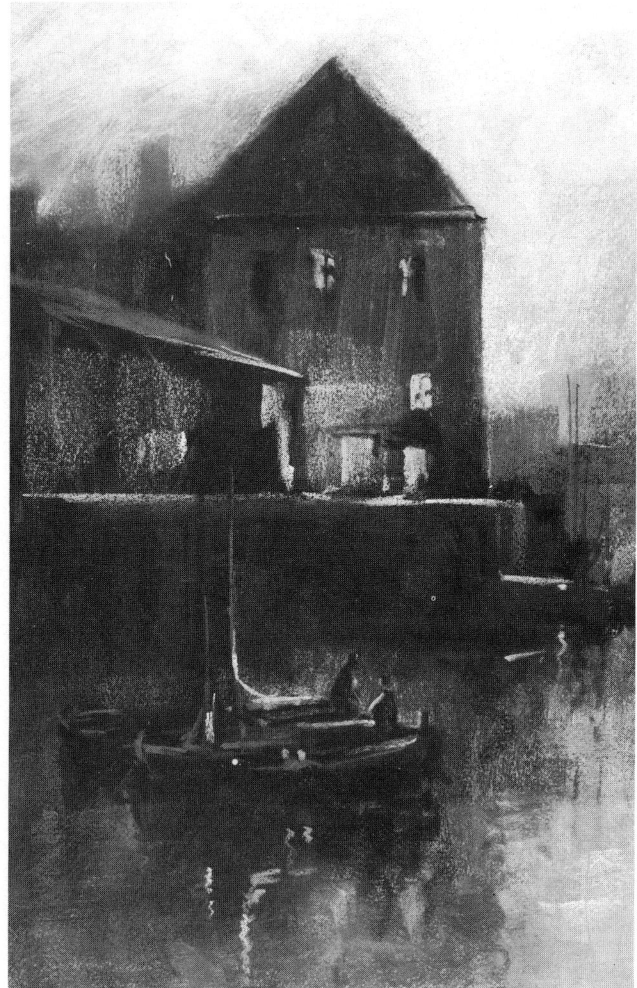

Black and white detail taken from the finished painting on page 29

Stage 1

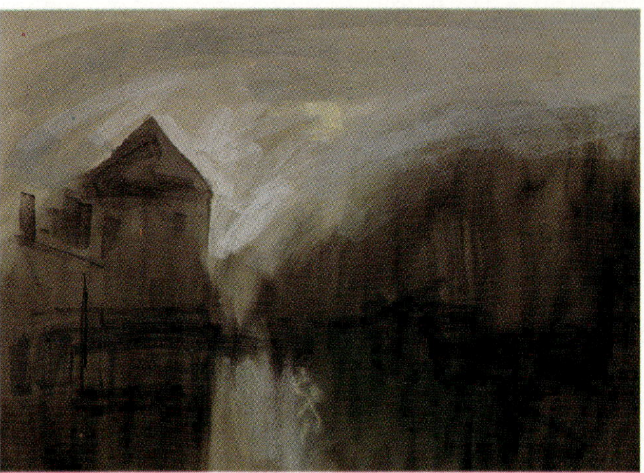
Stage 2

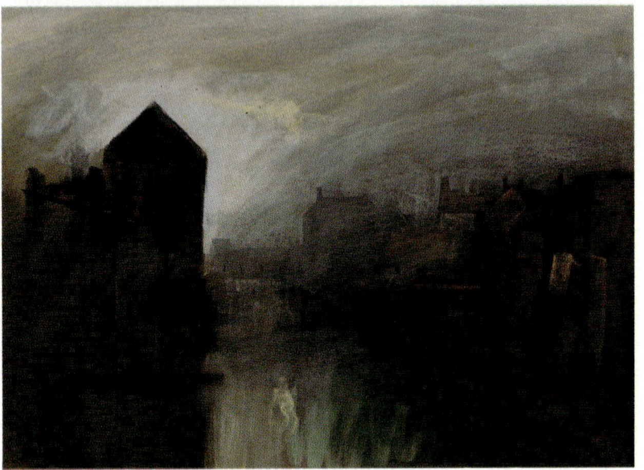
Stage 3

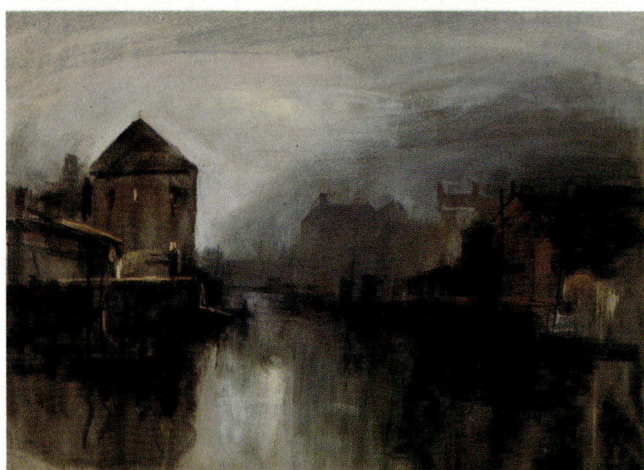
Stage 4

Stage 3

I further develop the sky, bringing in more light around the building on the left to give contrast, and follow with silhouetted shapes of blue-grey for distant buildings. Next, I introduce warmth into the picture with some mid-tones of burnt umber and Vandyke brown. Mid-warm grey and a little pale blue-grey suggest a feeling of soft light to the right of the distant buildings.

Stage 4

I now firm up the shapes of boats and buildings, introducing vague figures. With touches of mid-Vandyke brown I develop more form particularly on the left. The touches of light which I am now adding would not register anywhere near as bright on a lighter toned paper as they do on this background of dark ink.

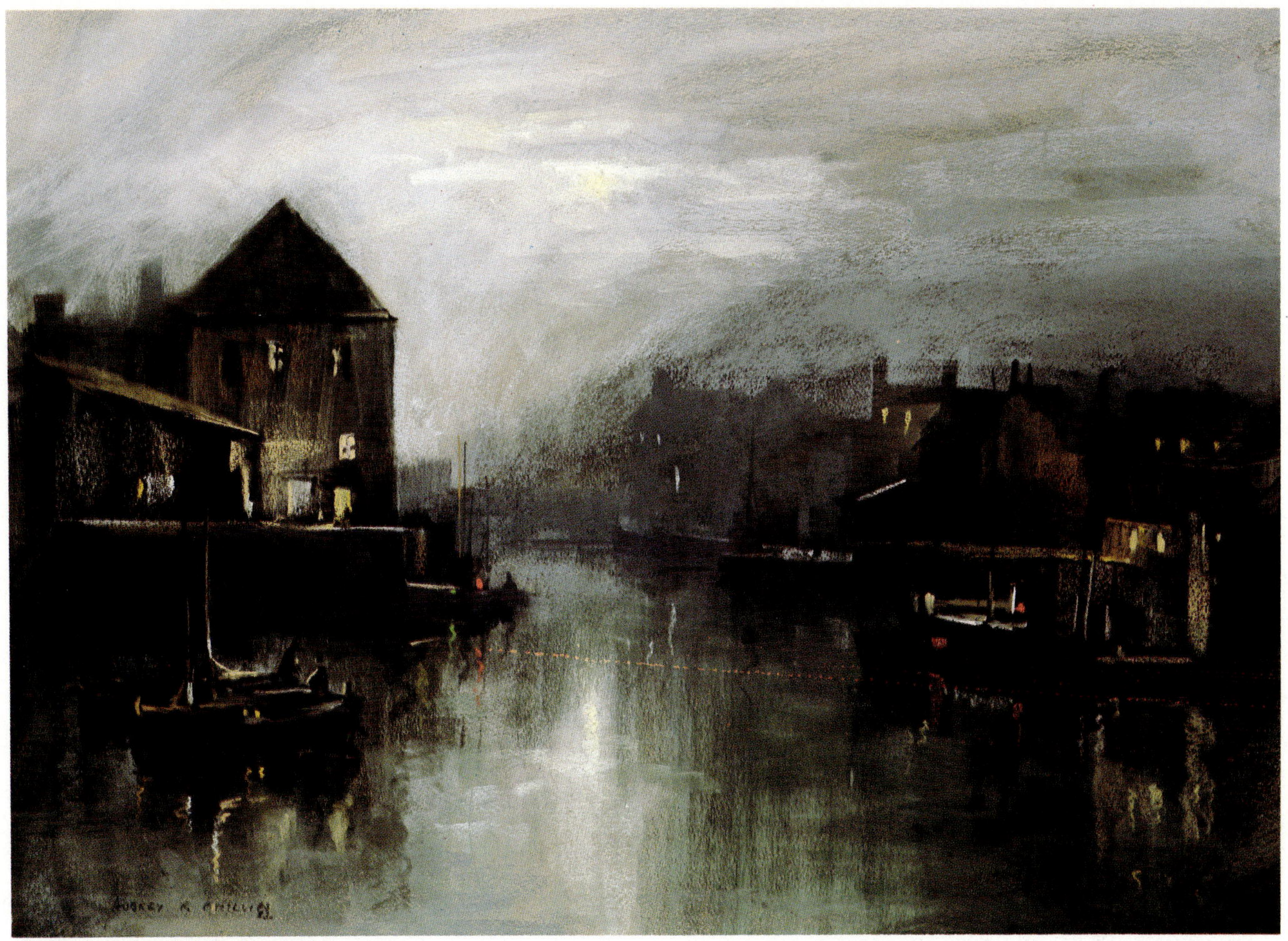

Stage 5 – the finished painting

Stage 5 – the finished painting

A general pulling-together of the whole composition now follows, the boats and buildings being worked up into more definition. I try not to lose the feeling of mystery and softness of my night-time subject. Brighter spots of colour, reds and greens of navigation lights on the boats and lighted windows complete the picture. The water of a harbour is never still, so the reflections of the lights in the picture become vertically elongated.

Sketching outdoors with pastel

Pastel is the ideal medium to take outdoors for sketching even if the results are later to be translated in the studio into more finished work in pastel, oils or watercolours. There are many advantages – firstly, very little cumbersome gear is needed. I use a piece of lightweight plywood approximately 16in. by 12in. (40cm by 30cm) as a drawing board, and onto this I clip my paper, either Canson, Ingres or sugar paper. I cut this to size by taking a full sized sheet 22in. by 30in. (53cm by 75cm) or 19in. by 24in. (47.5cm by 60cm), folding it in half and cutting along the fold. I then fold the half pieces but do NOT cut them.

I make my sketch on half of one of these pieces which leaves the other half to fold over to protect it. I find these paper sizes about right to enable me to put down (very quickly and broadly) what I feel are the essentials of a subject. I clip several sheets of paper onto my board as this gives me a nice firm pad to work on which is more pleasant than pressing directly onto the board. I choose chiefly greys, buffs or browns in various tones and hold them in position with strong bulldog clips so that they will not flap about in windy weather.

My broken pieces of pastel are carried in a flat airtight plastic sandwich box, which also contains flour about an inch deep to keep the sticks clean. I also take a sketch-book of smooth white cartridge paper about 14in. by 10in. (35cm by 25cm) and a few sticks of charcoal and conté crayon together with a putty rubber. With these I can make quick studies in black and white to supplement my pastel sketches. I also include a few felt tipped pens, both fine and broad points, all of which enable me to make more detailed studies if required in support of my pastel sketches. One or two soft pencils also are useful. I find that a damp cloth carried in a plastic bag can be used to clean up one's hands. I usually carry a small lightweight stool, but do not always use it as I often make do with what nature has to offer in the way of fallen trees or boulders to sit on. I do not find an easel necessary as I usually sit with my drawing board on my knees and my pastels within easy reach on the ground.

Incidentally, always use a waterproof container for your pastels: I remember once using a cardboard box and placing it on a wet beach, with the result that the pastels were ruined by the damp seeping from below without my realising it! All of my gear is contained (together with sandwiches and a Thermos flask) in a fisherman's bag which I sling over my shoulder, leaving me free to walk around in search of subject-matter. I prepare for adverse weather by carrying a plastic mac and studying the weather forecast before setting out.

River sketch (right)

By shifting my viewpoint only slightly to the right from where I was sitting for the demonstration on pages 3–5, I was able to obtain this vertical composition. I spend as much time looking for subjects as I do drawing or painting them – there are numerous compositions to be found just by turning on one spot through 360 degrees. This picture was painted with the same range of pastels as in the earlier demonstration.

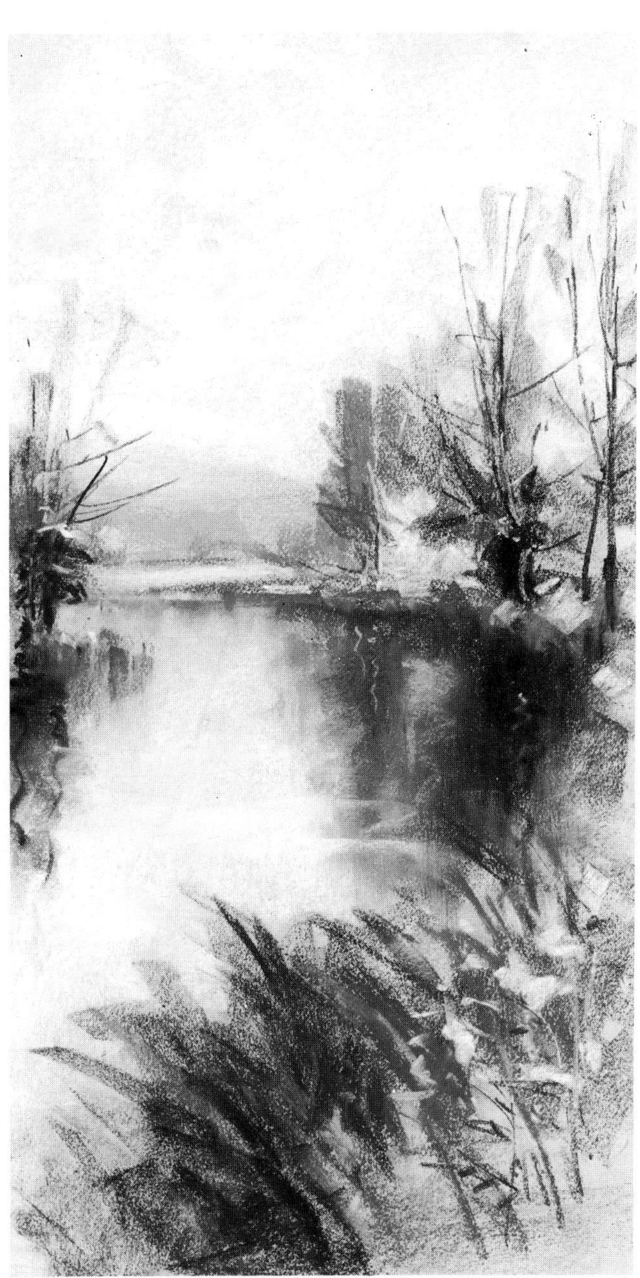

First published in Great Britain in 1984 by Search Press Limited,
Wellwood, North Farm Road, Tunbridge Wells, Kent TN2 3DR

Text, drawings and paintings by Aubrey Phillips

Reprinted 1988, 1990

U.S. Artists Materials Trade Distributor:
Winsor & Newton, Inc.
II, Constitution Avenue, P. O. Box 1396, Piscataway, NJ 08855-1396

Canadian Distributors:
Anthes Universal Limited
341 Heart Lake Road South, Brampton, Ontario L6W 3K8

Australian Distributors:
Jasco Pty. Limited
937-941 Victoria Road, West Ryde, N.S.W. 2114

New Zealand Distributors:
Caldwell Wholesale Ltd
Wellington and Auckland

ISBN 0 85532 531 3

Made and printed in Spain by Artes Graphicas Elkar, S. Coop.
Autonomía, 71 - 48012-Bilbao - Spain.

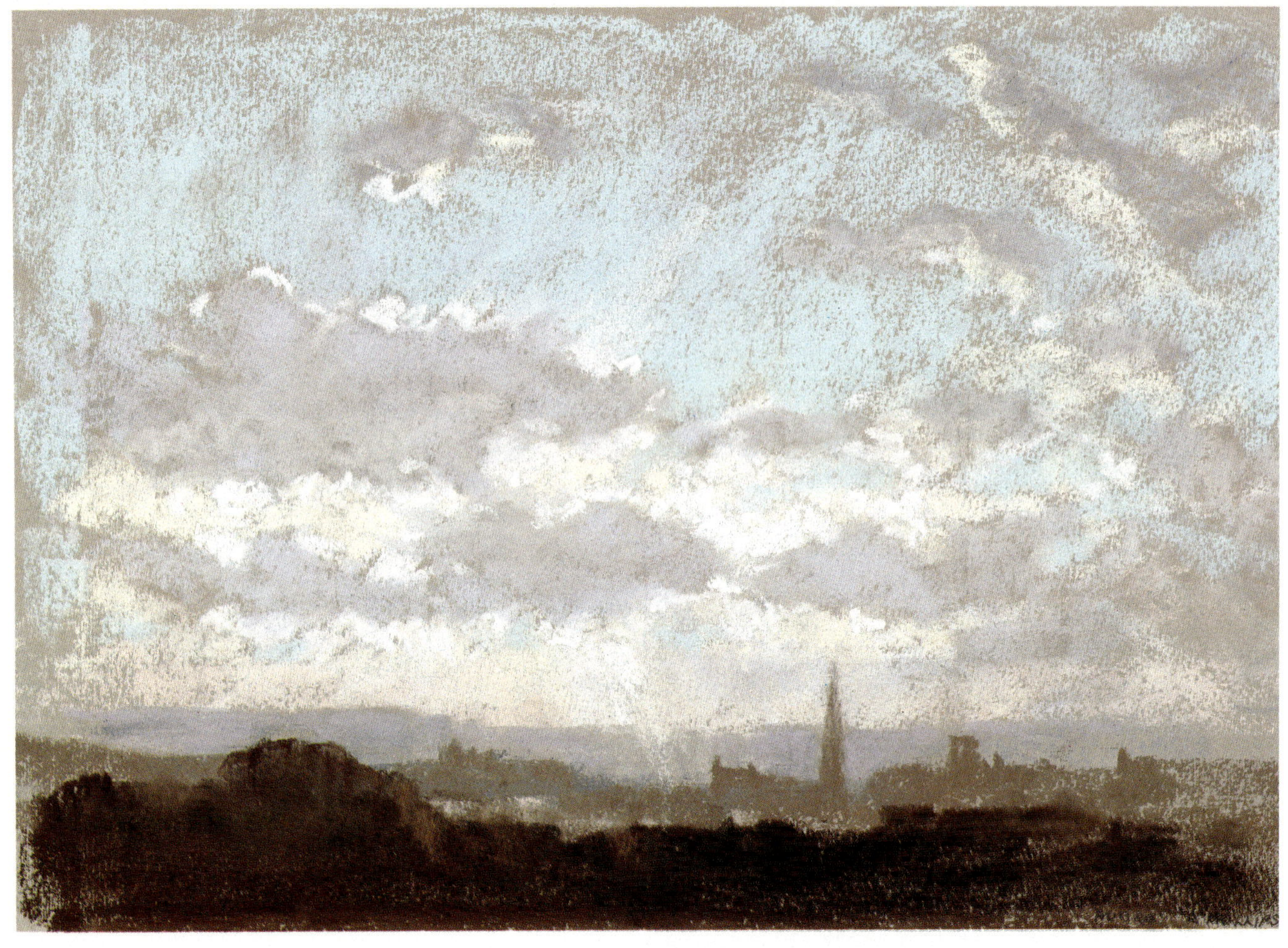

Silver lining *(above)*

This is the type of effect which we see early in the morning or during the late afternoon as we look towards the sun when it is low in the sky and partly hidden by broken cloud.

The greatest problem in dealing with this kind of subject is how to express brilliant light. The lightest pigment which we have at our disposal is white, so we have to adjust all the other tonal relationships in order to make the uttermost use of this light. In this study, the middle-toned grey Canson paper helped from the beginning. I use the palest tint of cerulean blue for the background and a darker grey for the clouds. The lightest clouds were pale yellow ochre with touches of white for the lightest parts and a little pale burnt sienna just above the horizon. The distant landscape was put in with a mid-toned blue-grey and a darker warm grey against it, with the darkest tone of sepia for the foreground. This darker passage helps to give contrast value to the lighter tonalities.